International Trade and Economic Co-operation

India's Approach and Perspectives

International Trade and Economic Co-operation

India's Approach and Perspectives

Gautam Murthy
Professor of Economics,
Centre for Indian Ocean Studies,
Osmania University, Hyderabad

New Century Publications
New Delhi, India

NEW CENTURY PUBLICATIONS
4800/24, Bharat Ram Road,
Ansari Road, Daryaganj,
New Delhi – 110 002 (India)

Tel.: 011-2324 7798, 4358 7398, 6539 6605
Fax: 011-4101 7798
E-mail: indiatax@vsnl.com • info@newcenturypublications.com
www.newcenturypublications.com

Editorial office:
LG–7, Aakarshan Bhawan,
4754-57/23, Ansari Road, Daryaganj,
New Delhi – 110 002

Tel.: 011-4356 0919

First Published: **July 2010**

ISBN: **978-81-7708-246-3**

Published by New Century Publications and printed at Salasar Imaging Systems, New Delhi.

Designs: Patch Creative Unit, New Delhi.

PRINTED IN INDIA

DEDICATED TO THE MEMORY OF MY DEAR FATHER

T.R.S MURTHY

Foreword

I have known Professor Gautam Murthy for the past twenty years, and am quite familiar with his academic writings and his views on global issues. He was on the Faculty of the Centre for Indian Ocean Studies, when I was the Director.

He has worked and published extensively on issues related to India's international trade, SAARC and ASEAN, both from strategic and economic perspectives. His scholarship and analytical skills are evident in the present volume. Professor Murthy has shown pragmatism in his work, and has taken into account new dimensions in India's foreign policy. He has provided useful insights and inputs which would prove useful to both academicians and policy formulators. The need to critically analyze the trends in international trade and economic co-operation cannot be overemphasized.

This book titled *International Trade and Economic Co-operation: India's Approach and Perspectives* by Professor Murthy should be useful to a cross-section of readership both in India and abroad.

Rama S. Melkote
(Formerly) Director, Centre for Indian Ocean Studies,
and Head, Department of Political Science,
Osmania University, Hyderabad

About the Book

India's geo-economics has undergone drastic changes after the initiation of economic reforms in the early 1990s. Prior to economic reforms, India had adopted a very cautious and guarded approach to regionalism.

Trade and economic co-operation with the countries of the world requires building up of shared infrastructure. Many Asian countries have joined together to develop cross-border infrastructure to lay the foundations for closer trading relationships and increased connectivity among countries.

Recognising that Regional Trade Agreements (RTAs) would continue to feature prominently in world trade, India has started engaging with its trading partners/blocks with the intention of expanding its export market and concluding trade and technology agreements and moving, in some cases, even towards Comprehensive Economic Cooperation Agreements (CECAs) which cover Free Trade Agreement (FTA) in goods, services, investments and identified areas of economic cooperation.

RTAs are an integral part of India's foreign trade policy, complementing the multilateral trading system. This book provides deep insights into India's trade and economic relations with regional groupings/blocks.

Author's Profile

Dr. Gautam Murthy is Professor of Economics at the Centre for Indian Ocean Studies, Osmania University, Hyderabad. He did his Ph.D. on "Trade and Export Instability in the ASEAN Economies" from the Gokhale Institute of Politics and Economics, Poona University. He was also Professor at XLRI, Jamshedpur. He has more than 25 years of teaching and research experience. His published books include *Regionalism in the Indian Ocean Rim*; *Strengthening Indo-South African Relations*; *Trade and Economic Co-operation*; and *International Economic Relations*. He has published more than 60 articles in leading Journals.

CONTENTS

Preface

Trade and economic co-operation with the countries of the world requires building up of shared infrastructure. Many Asian countries have joined together to develop cross-border infrastructure to lay the foundations for closer trading relationships and increased connectivity among countries.

Prior to economic reforms process initiated in 1991, India had adopted a very cautious and guarded approach to regionalism. Recognising that Regional Trade Agreements (RTAs) would continue to feature prominently in world trade, India has started engaging with its trading partners/blocks with the intention of expanding its export market and concluding trade and technology agreements and moving, in some cases, even towards Comprehensive Economic Cooperation Agreements (CECAs) which cover Free Trade Agreement (FTA) in goods, services, investments and identified areas of economic cooperation.

RTAs are an integral part of India's foreign trade policy, complementing the multilateral trading system. Framework agreements have already been entered into with a number of trading partners with specific road maps to be followed and specified time frames by which the negotiations are to be completed. Joint Study Groups have also been set up for examining feasibility of CECA between India-Japan, India-Brazil-South Africa and India-Russia. India and European Commission have also set up a High Level Trade Group (HLTG) as mandated by the India-EU Summit held in New Delhi on September 7, 2005. The mandate of the HLTG is to explore ways and means to increase bilateral economic flows including the possible launching of negotiations on a comprehensive trade and investment agreement.

East Asia—including Japan, China, South Korea and ASEAN—is today India's largest trading partner, ahead of EU and the US. India unveiled the *Look East* policy in 1991. Proliferation of Free Trade Agreements (FTAs) is the clearest evidence of Asian countries' desire to forge closer economic relationships. The growing importance of CECAs indicates that such agreements are becoming deeper, extending to areas beyond just tariff reduction.

The Agreement on SAARC Preferential Trading Arrangement (SAPTA) was signed during the 12th SAARC Summit on January 6, 2004 in Islamabad. The tariff liberalisation programme under the Agreement came into force from July 1, 2006.

India, Pakistan and Sri Lanka are categorized as Non-Least Developed Contracting States (NLDCS) and Bangladesh, Bhutan, Maldives and Nepal are categorized as Least Developed Contracting States (LDCS). Afghanistan which became the eighth member of SAARC during the 14th SAARC Summit held on April 3-4, 2007 in New Delhi is due to become a party to the SAFTA Agreement as an LDC member.

India's engagement with the Association of South East Asian Nations (ASEAN) started with its *Look East Policy* in the year 1991. ASEAN has a membership of 10 countries, namely Brunei Darussalam, Cambodia, Indonesia, Lao PDR, Malaysia, Myanmar, Philippines, Singapore, Thailand and Vietnam. India became a Sectoral Dialogue Partner of ASEAN in 1992 and Full Dialogue Partner in 1996. In November 2001, the ASEAN-India relationship was upgraded to the summit level.

India-Sri Lanka Free Trade Agreement, signed in December 1998 and in operation since March 2000, provides for tariff reduction/elimination in a phased manner on all items except the negative list and tariff rate quota (TRQ) items. Now, both sides are in advanced stage of negotiation on having a Comprehensive Economic Partnership Agreement (CEPA) which would encompass trade in goods as well as trade in services and economic cooperation.

The initiative to establish Bangladesh-India-Sri Lanka-Thailand Economic Cooperation (BIST-EC) was taken by

Thailand in 1994 to explore economic cooperation on a sub-regional basis involving contiguous countries of South East & South Asia grouped around the Bay of Bengal. Myanmar was admitted in December 1997 and the initiative was renamed as BIMSTEC. It may be mentioned that the initiative involves 3 members of SAARC (India, Bangladesh and Sri Lanka) and 2 members of ASEAN (Thailand, Myanmar). BIMSTEC is visualized as a *bridging link* between two major regional groupings, i.e. ASEAN and SAARC. BIMSTEC is an important element in India's *Look East* strategy and adds a new dimension to our economic cooperation with South East Asian countries.

The Comprehensive Economic Cooperation Agreement (CECA) between India and Singapore was signed on June 29, 2005 by the Prime Minister Mr. Manmohan Singh and Mr. Lee Hsien Loong, Prime Minister of Singapore. The CECA has become operational with effect from August 1, 2005.

In December 2007, India granted market access on additional 539 tariff lines through a Protocol amending the India-Singapore CECA. The implementation of CECA is reviewed regularly at the level of Secretaries.

I would like to place on record my deep appreciation to following persons for their help and co-operation over the years, both professionally and personally: Professor P.V.Rao, Director, Centre for Indian Ocean Studies, Osmania University, Hyderabad; Mr. A.N. Ram, (Formerly) Secretary (East), Ministry of External Affairs, Government of India; Professor Y. Yagama Reddy, Director, Centre for South East Asian and Pacific Studies, S.V. University, Tirupati; Vice Admiral Mihir Roy, Society for Indian Ocean Studies, New Delhi.

I sincerely thank my dear parents, brother, and wife for their constant support and encouragement over the years.

Hyderabad **Gautam Murthy**
June 2010

1

India-ASEAN Relations: Historical Perspectives and Looking Ahead

1.1 Introduction

ASEAN (Association of South East Asian Nations) is a political, economic and cultural organization of countries of South East Asia. The original signatories of ASEAN Declaration at Bangkok, signed in 1967 were Indonesia, Malaysia, the Philippines, Singapore and Thailand. The Sultanate of Brunei became a member in 1984. In mid-1995, Vietnam gained admission as the seventh member of ASEAN. Laos and Myanmar followed suit two years later in 1997, and Cambodia joined in 1999. Thus, ASEAN today has 10 members, covering all the countries of South East Asia from Myanmar in the extreme West to Vietnam in the extreme East. ASEAN has also emerged as a major force in international relations, with the ARF (ASEAN Regional Forum) given great importance by all great powers including China, the U.S, Russia and Japan. The high-profile EAS (East Asia Summits) consisting of ASEAN, China, India, Japan, South Korea. Australia and New Zealand also draw worldwide attention.

India has moved purposefully in developing a broad economic and strategic partnership with these dynamic countries of Southeast Asia. In pursuance of India's "Look East" policy, the dialogue has moved consistently forward from a sectoral-dialogue relationship in 1992, membership of the high-profile strategic forum ARF (ASEAN Regional Forum) in 1996, Indo-ASEAN summits since 2002, to the recently concluded (2009) Indo-ASEAN TIG (Trade in Goods) Agreement. In 2009, Indo-ASEAN trade was US$ 40 billion, and the target is to reach US$ 60 billion by 2010-2011.When ASEAN, China, Japan, and South Korea are included in the trade ambit of India, we gain strongly by more than US$ 20 billion annually. ASEAN in 2009 was India's fourth-largest trading partner, after the EU (European Union), US and China. Indo-ASEAN trade has been growing at a compounded annual rate of 28 percent since 2008-2009.

1.2 Territorial Ambit of Asia

Asia is essentially a geographical expression. It covers the Arabic-speaking countries in West Asia, Israel, Turkey and Iran, SAARC (including Afghanistan), South East Asia; and East Asia covering China, Japan and the Korean peninsula.

All the Asian countries comprise a variety of ethnic groups, languages and faiths. Historically there has been no evolution of an "Asian entity" or an "Asian identity". [1] This is in marked contrast to the unifying embrace of a Latin American identity, which brings the people of South and Central America together, a Caribbean identity, an African identity, a North American identity and a European identity. This sense of shared identity has already found institutional expression in the European Union, the Organization of American States, or the African Union (AU). In contrast, in Asia there are at least three large groupings—the Arabic-speaking countries of West Asia, SAARC and the ASEAN. The remaining countries remain territorially unaffiliated. The UN (United Nations) however divides Asia between its Arabic-speaking members in the Economic Commission for West Asia and all other Asian countries into ESCAP, which brings together the Asian countries with countries of the Pacific as well—ranging from Australia and New Zealand to diverse island countries of the Pacific like Togo and Vanuatu. It is only in the last few years of the last century and more so in the present century that one talks of a unified, 'Asian Century'.

The idea of Asia has also expanded so as now to include the Central Asian Republics of the former Soviet Union. [2] However, when one talks of an 'Asian Century', we only include member-states of ASEAN, China, Japan, Republic of Korea and India. West Asia, Central Eurasian countries (former Soviet Republics) and remaining member-countries of SAARC are ignored.

Asia is a region of multiple heterogeneities—geographic, economic, political and social. The region does not lack natural and human resources, but lacks initiatives for building complementarities. A closing of the ranks in the whole of Asia will ensure greater reciprocity in economic relations with Europe and North America. Often it is argued that the size and dynamism of the Asian economy is a potentially autonomous engine of growth, which need not exclusively depend on the health and policy imperatives of developed countries of Europe and North America. The Asian region as whole accounts today for 50 percent of global exports, 40 percent of global imports, and 60 percent of global international reserves. A dynamic Asian economy could compensate to a substantial degree for the sluggish growth elsewhere. [3] This growth potential derives from the large and diversified natural resource base and productive structures in the region. Its member countries produce everything from energy, vital minerals, tropical products, fibres and cereals. It covers industrial and trading capacities ranging from the most capital-intensive to the most labour-intensive, with a large and varied work force commanding different compensation levels. All these factors are highly conducive to a greater economic interaction. [4] Some strategic observers have even noted that it may be desirable to take even Pakistan on board in a future Asian alliance. Thus one could envisage a new Asian economic and strategic architecture including the East Asia Summit members SCO (Shanghai Cooperation Organization) members, as well as all other South, West and Central-Eurasian countries.

1.3 Regional Co-operation and Integration

Regional cooperation and integration are used

interchangeably in international trade literature today. The motivating factors for integration or more particularly, what is defined in the literature as, the Regional Trading Arrangements (RTAs) or Free Trade Agreements (FTAs) are the following:

- Regional cooperation can be effective in exploiting regional complementarities and economies of scale.
- Regional cooperation by bringing about diplomatic cohesion, can reduce regional tensions, and can be effective in keeping out negative extra-regional influences.
- Regional cooperation can lead to industrial restructuring and more efficient production structures within individual countries that is, efficiency-induced domestic industrial restructuring.
- Smaller countries can get increased 'security of market access' and 'safe havens' by forming RTAs.
- Unilateral domestic policy reforms can be locked-in, once RTAs are formed.
- Countries in RTAs can improve their bargaining power in MTNs (Multilateral Trade Negotiations).
- Industries can be promoted that are not viable without protected regional markets that is, regional infant industries; the idea being that they would be internationally competitive if given sufficient time to develop.
- RTAs can offer quicker solution for freer world trade than multilateralism, which is slower process.
- Article 24 of WTO views RTAs are being consistent with globalization.
- Intra-regional trade liberalization increases competition for industries of the region, improves technical and business complementarity and also attracts FDI.

1.4 Asian Regional Organizations

The major regional organizations in Asia, besides ASEAN, are:

- The GCC (Gulf Cooperation Council), which was established in 1981 and has six Arab states namely, Bahrain, Kuwait, Oman, Qatar, Saudi Arabia and UAE as members.
- SAARC, established in 1985, comprises eight countries-Bangladesh, Bhutan, India, Maldives, Nepal, Pakistan, Sri Lanka and, since 2007, Afghanistan.
- IOR-ARC (Indian Ocean Rim Association for Regional Cooperation) was established in 1997 with as many as nineteen countries as its members. The key players are Australia, India and South Africa.
- SCO (Shanghai Cooperation Organization) includes China, Russia and the five Central Asian Republics of Kyrgyzhistan, Kazakhstan, Turkmenistan, Tajikistan and Uzbekistan are members. Pakistan, Iran and India are observers.
- APEC (Asia Pacific Economic Cooperation forum) formed in 1993 is based on the idea of 'open regionalism'. Voluntary action and consensual decisions form the basis of cooperation. It is a regional non-starter, too diverse, geographically scattered, and no meaningful integration. The areas of voluntary action envisioned include trade liberalization; trade facilitation; investment facilitation; and sectoral cooperation projects.

Today, over 70 percent of world trade is routed through RTAs FTAs or PTAs (Preferential Trading Agreements), and around 40 percent through multilateral or MFN (Most Favoured Nation) process. There are over 200 RTAs/FTAs in the world.

1.5 India-ASEAN Linkages: Chronology

1. 1991: India's engagement with ASEAN started with its "Look East Policy"
2. 1992: India became a Sectoral Dialogue Partner of ASEAN-Cooperating in Trade, Investment and Tourism.
3. 1996: India became a Full Dialogue Partner and an active

participant in the ARF.ARF met for the first time in 1994.

4. 2001: ASEAN-INDIA relationship upgraded to the summit level.
5. 2002: First ASEAN-INDIA Summit.
6. 2003: Second ASEAN-INDIA Summit concluded with the signing of three major documents:

- Framework Agreement for Comprehensive Economic Cooperation.
- Accession Document to the TAC (Treaty of Amity and Co-operation).
- Adoption of the Joint Declaration on Cooperation in Combating International Terrorism.

7. 2004: Third ASEAN-India Summit. Agreement on "India-ASEAN Partnership for Peace, Progress and Shared Prosperity".
8. 2005: Fourth ASEAN-INDIA Summit. India's high profile role established in the East Asia Summit, with ASEAN, Japan, Korea, China, Australia and New Zealand. (16 countries). India has an FTA with Thailand and A (Comprehensive Economic Cooperation Agreement was signed with Singapore in 2005.
9. 2006, 2007, and 2008: Fifth, Sixth, and Seventh ASEAN-India Summits were held. Considerable further progress was made in closer economic integration with these countries, at these Summits.

1.6 India-ASEAN FTA (Free Trade Area)

In August 2009 India signed a FTA with ASEAN. The FTA is considered a significant achievement by India into a formidable regional trade bloc. Tariff liberalization for a large number of products traded will be substantially reduced. The TIG (Trade in Goods) Agreement focuses on mutually agreed tariff lines from both sides and is targeted to eliminate tariffs on 80 percent of tariff lines accounting for 75 percent of trade in a gradual manner from January 2010. The agreement also provides flexibility to India and ASEAN to exclude some products from tariff eliminations. India has excluded 489 items from the list of tariff concessions and 590 items from the list of tariff eliminations. India and ASEAN are also finalizing a "Trade in Services and Investment" agreement, expected to be signed by the end of 2009. India stands to gain substantially from this agreement, as it will provide greater access to the services market in ASEAN, where India has acknowledged strengths.

There are two other sub-regional partnerships, which India has in the ASEAN region. These are:

- MGC (Mekong-Ganga Cooperative Forum) floated by India with 5 of its Eastern neighbours-Myanmar, Thailand, Cambodia, Vietnam and Laos in 2001. Tourism, culture and education are given precedence and priority in the cooperative framework. Transport, communication, and infrastructure are next areas of priority.
- BIMSTEC (Bay of Bengal Initiative for Multi-Sectoral Technical and Economic Cooperation). It is part of India's immediate and intermediate neighbourhood policy and includes: 1. India 2. Bangladesh 3. Bhutan 4. Myanmar 5. Thailand 6. Nepal 7. Cambodia 8. Vietnam and 9. Laos.
- The Mekong basin has the potential to emerge as a major granary as its vast lands are very fertile. India and Thailand can do much to tame the Mekong River, and enhance cultivation by spreading irrigation.

1.7 India and South East Asia: Civilizational Perspectives

An unfortunate fact of history is that despite strong civilizational ties with South East Asia dating back to centuries, and despite the Indian diaspora scattered around many countries of the ASEAN region, India failed in its efforts to befriend the countries of the region in the recent past.

India's first contacts with Southeast Asia began in the Maurayan dynasty, when emissaries of Ashoka spread Buddhism across the region. In the first century AD, the migration of Indian princes, priests, poets and artisans triggered off cultural efflorescence in South East Asian countries. The greatest temples of Vishnu are located not in India, but in South East Asia-like the Angkor Vat- Siam Rep complex in Cambodia, and the biggest Buddha stupa in Boru Budur in Indonesia.

The second phase began with the growth of maritime trade with South East Asia. The Gujarati Muslim merchants, mainly subscribing to the Sufi variant of Islam, played an important role in the Islamisation of Malay peninsula and the Indonesian archipelago. It is primarily for this reason that Islam in South East Asia is more accommodative and "malleable" than the exclusionary Wahabi type of Islam of West Asia. The great sea-faring kings of the 12th century in India established the Khmer and Sri Vijaya empires. In the colonial times, the vast reservoir of Indian manpower was exploited to serve the colonial interests of Britain. The rubber plantations in Malaya, the backbone of the Malayan economy, and the sugar plantations in the far-flung areas of the British Empire were developed as a result of the exploitation of Indian workers. Today there are 4.5 million people of Indian origin in South East Asia. They constitute 8 percent of the population of Malaysia and 7 percent of the population of Singapore.

Some useful facts highlighting the close civilizational contacts between India and Malaysia are instructive:

- The Ramayana in its variations is the national epic of both Indonesia and Thailand.
- The King of Thailand, a Buddhist country, traces his origin to Rama, and is considered the 9th incarnate of Rama.
- The symbol "Ganesha" is embossed on the Indonesian Rupaiah.
- Many words of Indian/Sanskrit origin are found in South East Asia. Singapore comes from "Singhapura" or Lion City. Brunei comes from the word Braun or "Varun", the Hindu God. The PM of Malaysia is called "Prathan Mantri", as are many other words in "Basha Malaya".
- Modern day Orissa still commemorates, the great Kalinga

kings conquests in modern-day Indonesia by a festival called Bali Jatra, where tiny boats with lamps on them are allowed to sail from the coast of Orissa.

- In modern times, the President of Singapore, Mr. Nathan is of Indian (Tamil origin), as are Cabinet ministers of Malaysia. The Orissa leader Biju Patnaik gave the name of a former Indonesian President "Megawati" Sukarnoputri.

ASEAN and India are today geographically contiguous, as Myanmar shares a long border with the North East States of India. The Southernmost tip of Andaman and Nicobar Islands, Indira Point, is just 40 km. from Aceh in Indonesia. The effect of this was adequately demonstrated in the Tsunami, when the Andaman's were more seriously affected than even other parts of Indonesia.

Independent India's engagement with Asia began under Jawaharlal Nehru. Under Nehru's leadership, the Asian Relation's Conference was organized in 1947, and the special conference on Indonesia in 1949.India also played an important role in organizing the Bandung Conference on Afro-Asian solidarity in 1955. Such was India's stature that India was given Chairmanship of the International Control Commission of Vietnam, Laos and Cambodia in 1954, as per the Geneva Agreement, which was supposed to unify North and South Vietnam after the French left Indo-China.

1.8 India and ASEAN: Geo-political Realities

However, India gradually began to get disillusioned with Asia, as the U.S began to isolate India with regional pacts like CENTO and SEATO. The Chinese also began to get overassertive, and India's complete disillusionment of playing a greater role in Asia, came with the Sino-Indian war of 1962. The Pakistan aggression of 1965, also made India turn away from her immediate neighbourhood. India at the same time began forging close ties both politically and economically with the Soviet Union. It must be admitted that the Soviet Union played a stellar role in shaping India's infrastructure, by helping India build her steel plants and large irrigation dams (which Nehru called the "Temples of Modern India"), the benefits of which India is reaping even today. Also, the Soviet Union helped India politically and in the defence sphere, and was a timely ally in India's moments of crisis. The defence relationship continues even today, with more than 70 percent of our defence equipment still coming from Russia. Modern Russia-a mineral, petroleum and gas rich Superpower will continue to be in India's strategic focus, despite India's diplomatic closeness with the United States, after the Indo-US Nuclear Agreement.

India's geo-political and more so geo-economic compulsions of allying with the FSU (Former Soviet Union), and away from Asia in the 1960s and 1970s must thus be viewed in its totality. Such was Nehru's disillusionment with Asia, that when Tunku Abdul Rahman, the former Prime Minister of Malaysia, and Lee Kuan Yew, the former Prime Minister of Singapore, approached him with the idea of forming an economic alliance with South East Asia, he tersely told them-"I have nothing to do with the Cocoa Cola economies". Prime Minister Indira Gandhi, also assiduously forged ties with the Indo-Chinese States, particularly Vietnam in the cold-war days. Support for India's association with the expanded ASEAN region is readily forthcoming because of Indira Gandhi's initiatives in the 1970s and 1980s. Rajiv Gandhi also played a role in renewing ties with Asia, with his path-breaking visit to China in 1988. His hand-shake with the legendary Chinese leader Deng Xiao Ping, set of a chain-reaction in restructuring Sino-Indian and India-Asia relations.

India initially perceived the establishment of ASEAN as an extension of the American sphere of influence. It viewed the origin of ASEAN as being political in its nature using regional economic co-operation merely as a rational for justifying its existence. The ASEAN countries viewed India as a satellite of the former Soviet Union. India's pro-Soviet line of handling its foreign policy on Vietnam and Cambodia in the

1970s and 1980s irked most of the ASEAN countries, and added to the political distance between India and ASEAN.

1.9 India-ASEAN: Economic Dimensions

India's relatively closed economy before 1990 also did not provoke interest among ASEAN, which had changed their strategies since the early 1970s towards outward-looking and more open economies. Lee Kuan Yew even advised Indira Gandhi "you may be non-aligned, but align yourself with the international market grid, and gate crash into the free market".

With the collapse of the Berlin Wall in 1989, and the disintegration of the Soviet Union soon after, the political freeze in relations between India and ASEAN made no sense. The improvement of India's relations with China since the mid-1980s, also improved the political environment in the ASEAN countries for strengthening economic co-operation with India. India's post-1991 economic reforms transformed the Indian economy to an attractive destination for expanding and diversifying the market for ASEAN exports. This has been very nicely put by Thomas Friedman in his book, "The World is Flat", in the chapter "When the Walls Came Down, and the Windows Went Up". [5]

The ASEAN countries also discovered several new complementarities among their economies, and the Indian economy. The surplus capital of some of the ASEAN countries could be put to good economic use by combining it with the globally recognized skills of scientific, technical, professional, and managerial manpower of India. India's defence capabilities, non-aggressive historical record and commitment to maintenance of peace in the world and in Asia are recognized.

The combined effect of the fundamentally altered economic, political and strategic environment in the ASEAN region, led the ASEAN grouping to clearly recognize the mutual benefits of strengthening economic relations with India.

The foundations of India's "Look East" policy were laid by Prime Minister P.V. Narasimha Rao. His famous Singapore lecture of 1994 in which he announced India's intention to use the Asia-Pacific region "as a spring board for India's leap into the global market-place" ushered in India's new engagement with Asia. The "Look East" initiatives are now pursued with renewed vigour, and today what we need is a "Focus East" policy. Today, India's "Gaze" towards ASEAN is so strong, that China and the United States are beginning to get wary of us.

The next step for India is to look beyond the ASEAN-East Asian region, and extend the policy to the vast Asia-Pacific region. It should also cover besides economic, strategic and socio-cultural issues as well. There is much scope for further expanding and deepening our co-operative agenda, synergizing the economies of India and the ASEAN and exploring new avenues for diplomatic complementarities.

India-ASEAN co-operation has progressed substantially in many spheres-mainly in science and technology, tourism, trade and investment. The level of investment flows on both sides also has progressed substantially, but still has a lot of untapped potential.

1.10 Geo-economics of Indo-ASEAN Engagement

The relevance of geo-economic relations as the dominant force in shaping the future of international and regional relations is most likely to grow substantially in the 21st century-notwithstanding the expanding role of WTO. In this noticeably altered global and regional context, economic diplomacy will increasingly overshadow the traditional political and geo-strategic dimensions of the foreign policy formulations of the decades to come. A coalitional approach to the management of power relations at the regional levels is most likely to be preferred in the economic sphere. The future battles arising from conflicts of national interests are most likely to be fought in the global regional markets, rather than on battlefields.

While small-scale or domestic conflicts are undermining peace and security of almost every sub-region in the Indian Ocean, large-scale regional security and strategic matters are also gaining in primacy, including the rise of terrorism. The large foreign military presence, the proliferation of weapons of mass destruction and missile capabilities, the security of sea lanes of communications (SLOCs), as well as smuggling and piracy at sea are getting increasing attention. In the pacific resolution of domestic conflicts, negotiation takes place in specific case-by-case forums, rather than in large multilateral region-wide organizations. Some Indian oceanic multilateral commitments on peace and security issues could certainly help to limit conflict escalation and their negative impact at the sub-regional scale. [6]

Within its three specific protocols, and its regional forum, the ASEAN Regional Forum (ARF) addressing peace, security and stability issues, ASEAN has developed an original framework that could certainly serve as a model for the development of a formal Indian oceanic co-operation on these matters.

It is thus obvious that regional co-operation in peace, security, and strategic matters could help limit ongoing conflict situations, prevent new conflicts, promote disarmament and non-proliferation, and address the role of foreign militaries in the region, thus generating a more stable geo-political environment. [7]

India has recently consciously attempted to provide explicit economic orientation to its foreign policy—the "Look East" policy for consciously expanding its economic linkages with ASEAN countries.

India's key position at the head of the Indian Ocean, astride the East-West trade route is n asset. Today, India's strategic influence stretches to both the entry points to the Indian Ocean—from the Straits to the Indian Ocean—from the Straits of Hormuz in the West, to the Straits of Mallaca in the

East.

The bulk of India's foreign trade is seaborne; besides protecting its long coastline and SLOCs, it has to adequately patrol her 200km EEZ (Exclusive Economic Zone), where there is frequent poaching by modern and fast South East Asian vessels. Threats from Pakistan and more recently the growing menace of the Chinese Navy, which has started making its presence felt in the Indian Ocean region through the Coco islands in the North Andamans Sea, are increasing.

India considers the Indian Ocean region well within its sphere of influence—and thus trade with the South East Asian countries-now all part of the ASEAN—assumes added importance in the emerging geo-economic strategies of India. Indo-ASEAN co-operation can serve as a stabilising factor in promoting India's geo-strategic interests in the Indian Ocean region.

1.11 India-ASEAN Co-operation in Emerging Area

There is much scope for further expanding and deepening our cooperative agenda, synergising the economies of India and ASEAN and exploring new avenues for diplomatic complementarities. [8]

India-ASEAN cooperation has progressed substantially in many spheres- mainly in science and technology, IT and electronics, HRD, transport and infrastructure, space technology, tourism and trade and investment. These initiatives are however not adequately reflected in trade figures. [9]

The level of investment flows on both sides has a lot of untapped potential and can easily rise to US$ 3 billion by 2010 with sustained efforts by both sides. The redeeming fact is that there are substantial investments by both India and ASEAN in each other's countries.

Although there have been significant changes in commodity composition of India's trade with ASEAN countries in recent years, components of the trade basket could do with substantial revision, with an increasing emphasis on India moving up the value chain.

India should also intensify its marketing thrust to ASEAN countries to correct the asymmetry in trade relations. Both infrastructure and technology can be hawked much more aggressively. Our exporters should negotiate much harder, offer more competitive terms, adhere to delivery schedules, and provide effective after-sales service. A marketing culture among our exporters, combined with a bit of hard sell, could help India make decisive inroads into the ASEAN markets.

Intensive efforts to promote business synergies on the two sides in areas such as infrastructure, IT, biotechnology, and tourism got a positive boost with the India-ASEAN Business Summits. A trade pact with ASEAN is the best beginning since India has traditionally enjoyed many links-economic and strategic- with the region, although there is a lot of untapped potential. We should also try to strengthen strategic alliances with the *guanxi (*overseas Chinese networks) who control most of the distribution channels in Malaysia, Singapore and to some extent Thailand. [10]

India should also make available information on its capabilities in fields like IT, and market these better in countries like the Philippines and Brunei, as trade with these two ASEAN countries is virtually non-existent.

The terms of India-ASEAN engagement needs to be taken much more seriously. The possibilities for functional cooperation are limitless, and enthusiasm should translate into tangible gains. Tourism, culture and education are given precedence and priority in the cooperative framework. Transport, communications and infrastructure will be prioritised in the next phase. The MGC also provides immense opportunities for India's private sector to create a niche in the region; India can make up for its past mistakes. Indo-ASEAN cooperation in tourism, culture and education can also be strengthened in Indonesia and Malaysia. [11]

It must be remembered that India's cultural footprints in

Southeast Asia have been left because of trade and religion, and not a show of power.

India's relations with ASEAN assume significance also in the light of the various cultural similarities it shares with the region. Buddhism is the natural link to S-E Asia, particularly the Mekong basin. The cultural ties with S-E Asia need to be stressed apart from trade and Buddhism.

ASEAN can also source its manpower requirements-technical and managerial- from India, as manpower here is both competitive and culturally compatible. Indian professionals teaching English and computer skills can raise the standards of education and knowledge base. The ASEAN-India HRD programme needs to-be further strengthened.

1.12 India-ASEAN Transportation Linkages

India has today got a new dimension to its Look- east vision -developing its north-eastern states by linking them to South East Asia through road and rail links via Myanmar. It is part of a larger project to build Eurasian land and rail corridors that could connect Singapore to Istanbul and Europe via both India and China. The Trans-Continental highway and railway could lead to the ultimate link up of China, Russia and Central Asia, bringing immense benefits to all the countries.

India recently opened the road linking Manipur's Tamu on the border with Myanmar with Kalewa and Kaleymo and from there to Mandalay-the commercial heart of Myanmar.

China has already agreed in principle to build a highway connecting Bangkok with Kunming in the thriving Yunan province of China, through Laos. A road from Kunming to Ruihi on the Chinese border with Myanmar already exists. China is also developing the "Irrawady Corridor" beginning in Kunming and reaching the Western Coast of Myanmar facing the Indian Ocean Rim. China's interior provinces such as Yunnan, Sichuan and Gizhou will no longer have to depend on far away ports on China's eastern sea-board and can have access to the warm waters of the Indian Ocean. Thailand also has plans to build another highway linking it with Vietnam through Laos. That will give Thailand access to the Danang port on the Vietnamese coastline. To the East, Thailand hopes to connect this road to Moulmein in Myanmar.

There is also a possibility of building a railway line between the Chinese cities of Kunming and Mytikyima on the Myanmar border, where both the roads, Ledo to Patakai Range and Ledo to South Myanmar meet. The Asian Development Bank has given a loan to the Myanmar government to construct the railway through northern Myanmar linking India with China. India thus wants to develop her northeast by using Myanmar as a bridge to economically leverage with China and the other ASEAN nations.

The essence of this triangular road and rail diplomacy among India, China, Myanmar and Thailand is also about ultimately about linking the Indian Ocean to the South China Sea. The Mekong basin also has the potential to emerge as a major granary as its vast lands are very fertile. India and Thailand can do much to tame the Mekong River, and enhance cultivation by spreading irrigation.

1.13 India-ASEAN: Human Resource Development (HRD)

ASEAN and India are jointly committed to conducting expert studies on Indian and ASEAN capabilities and complementarities in this sector. Academic exchange programmes, India Study Centres in ASEAN, ASEAN Study Centres in India, Linking Indian Universities with the ASEAN University Network (AUN), possibility of ASEAN placements in IITs and IIMs.

An ASEAN-India Eminent Persons Lecture Series was launched with the objective of promoting awareness about the reality and potential of ASEAN-India partnership. This programme is coordinated by RIS (Research and Information System for Non-Aligned Countries), a Government of India sponsored think-thank based in New Delhi. Eminent leaders and opinion makers, senior academics, media personalities, technologists, captains of trade and industry are invited to give public lectures on different aspects of economic, political, cultural and security ties between ASEAN countries and India.

1.14 India-ASEAN: Synergies and the Way Ahead

In economic and strategic terms India wants to develop its north east by increasing its connectivity with the rest of the world through commercial linkages with ASEAN. By taking advantage of Myanmar's links with other ASEAN countries, India hopes to transform the northeast from a *security burden* into a *land of economic opportunity.* [12]

The Mekong basin also has the potential to emerge as a major granary as its vast lands are very fertile. India and Thailand can do much to tame the Mekong River, and enhance cultivation by spreading irrigation.

ASEAN also faces the problem of disparity in development, the new entrants—Laos, Vietnam and Cambodia showing lower levels of performance compared to the other members-and will take time to integrate fully into the ASEAN framework. India can offer its help here as well by providing interest-free credit facilities for speedier development of these countries, and cashing in on the tremendous good-will that existed for her in the cold-war days.

There is also immense scope for further enhancing joint ventures in manufacturing, consultancy, leasing and trading outfits between India and ASEAN. The Indian bureaucracy is continuing to give explicit economic orientation to its foreign policy.

At the geo-political level, India's membership of the ARF (ASEAN Regional Forum), discussing security issues, can serve to effectively protect and project India's strategic interests in the region. While India's membership of ARF enables it to participate in regional security issues, we would seriously undermine our long term strategic and economic interests, if we do not take into account China's rapidly expanding economic and strategic profile in our eastern neighbourhood. [13]

The second phase of India's Look East policy also coincides with India's *dalliance* with the U.S, as opposed to a formal *alliance*. India today has more intensive security links with America's allies in the ARF (Asian Regional Forum of ASEAN)-Australia, South Korea and Japan. India's improved ties with the U.S have also created the space for a more confident and constructive engagement with China in both strategic and economic terms. India's "Look East" policy should also be integrated into a larger regionalization strategy, encompassing South Asia, the Indian Ocean Rim, the Bay of Bengal Rim, and the Asia-Pacific. As SAARC continues to remain moribund because of the ego clashes in the region, and the IOR-ARC faces teething problems and is yet to take off, India's future lies in having a definite focus eastwards-particularly with ASEAN-and strengthening the infrastructural, economic, cultural and commercial relations with these countries.

India's new found enthusiasm to forge a trade pact with ASEAN also stands in stark contrast with its attitude towards SAARC, and even towards bilateral relations with its neighbours in South Asia. That a free trade area in South Asia remains a non-starter is not entirely the fault of Pakistan-India too has been reluctant to make the larger concessions that will make a more effective South Asian grouping.

The East Asia summit (EAS) had sixteen countries attending; the ASEAN ten, South Korea, Japan, India, China, Australia, and New Zealand. EAS may ultimately evolve into an East Asian Community (EAC) discussing economic and strategic issues. EAC may finally subsume the evolving ASEAN community, to form a larger Asian economic grouping.

No country, particularly China should be allowed to dominate any future visions of an Asian Community, by practicing a "Monroe Doctrine for Asia", seeking absolute influence over the entire East Asian region.

In conclusion, India will need to be strong economically if it has to be recognized as a major regional or global power. Closer economic and political interaction with the economically dynamic group of countries like ASEAN will motivate our decision makers to effect much needed changes in economic institutions and policies to make the economy vibrant and foreign policy more dynamic.

ASEAN has a combined economy bigger than India or South Korea and a total population of over half a billion people. It has the potential to become an economic force that could rival China, India, Brazil and Russia. The absence of ASEAN from investors' radar screens as a unified economic unit is due to lack of integration of the bloc's economies and financial markets. Both local and international investors still widely view the South-East Asian region as 10 separate economies due to differences in regulations, business environment, institutional capacity, and culture. Thus further integration of ASEAN is necessary in order to maximize intra-regional synergies and keep the region relevant to the international economy and investors.

ASEAN has earned its way to the global high table. Its member countries have weathered the financial storm well. Economic activity did contract in some open economies such as Singapore, Thailand and Malaysia, but the worst is over, and their economies and financial systems have suffered no collateral damage. Indonesia and Vietnam are emerging as Asia's two outperformers. ASEAN's purchasing power could double by 2023, creating significant opportunities in consumer products and services.

ASEAN economies have built up their resilience through years of reforms and restructuring since the Asian financial crisis of 1997-98. The accumulation of foreign exchange reserves has helped maintain investor confidence and limit undue volatility while a well-capitalized banking sector has been critical to ensuring the smooth running of the region's economy. Indeed, the ASEAN region has all the ingredients to become a global economic force. In 2008, its 10 members had a combined GDP of US$ 1.5 trillion, 580 million people, and total trade of US$ 1.7 trillion (26 percent of it intra-regional). If ASEAN were a single-country, it would be the world's 10th largest economy, and the third most populous country. Counting only extra-regional trade, ASEAN is the world's fifth-largest trading power, after the US, Germany, China and Japan. In recent years ASEAN's free-trade agreements with China, India, Japan, and South Korea have deepened the region's economic links with the rest of Asia.

ASEAN as a combined economy would rank among the world's top 10 in terms of FDI inflows. Fears of China taking every FDI dollar from ASEAN have not been matched by reality. ASEAN still managed to attract US$ 60 billion of FDI in 2008,with intra-regional investment accounting for a sizable portion as foreign investors, especially from within Asia, see countries such as Indonesia and Vietnam as alternative manufacturing bases as the cost of doing business in China rises. The region's economic integration is still at an early stage and much work is required to remove barriers to the trade of goods and the free flow of capital, information and talent. These measures are relevant to businesses as they enhance access to the whole ASEAN consumer market from any one member country.

Amid the rise of China and India, there are ongoing concerns that some of the South-East Asian nations may be marginalised. This is primarily a result of the economic and political diversity of ASEAN members. For example, the World Bank's "Doing Business Survey, 2010" ranks Singapore as the easiest place in the world to do business, while it ranks Laos 177th out of 181 countries. Politically, ASEAN's members range from Indonesia, the world's third largest democracy (after the U.S and India), to Myanmar at the other end of the spectrum. Brunei's economy is heavily dependent on oil and gas. Thailand; Vietnam, Indonesia and Malaysia have considerable agricultural production bases. By contrast, Singapore has few, if any, natural resources, and relies on imports for local consumption and manufacturing, financial services and trading drives its economy.

Clearly, ASEAN's smaller members need a common platform to represent their interests and ASEAN could become that key channel through which these members can make their voices heard on the global stage. The challenge for ASEAN leaders at their fifteenth summit in Thailand is to convince the business sector and investors that ASEAN is a workable concept. The plan to establish an ASEAN Economic Community by 2015, while ambitious, is necessary to push the region's integration forward.

The FTA with ASEAN is an economic "win win" for both sides, although its merit lies more on its political and diplomatic impact on ASEAN. During negotiations lasting over six years when India dithered many times, an impression gathered in ASEAN countries that India was not serious about engaging Asia. Signing the FTA has signalled India's commitment to economic integration and political cooperation with South East Asia as a logical outcome of its Look East policy (LEP).

The main thrust of our South East Asia policy being economic integration and energy security, LEP has less of a political, strategic or cultural dimension. Given India's effort to integrate with the global economy, diplomacy focuses more on trade and investment. India's LEP lacks a strategic vision of a future Asia Pacific that can inform its policies and actions, helping it establish its rightful place in the Asian balance of power. Such failure to articulate a vision is pervasive of foreign policy in its entirety as India faces new challenges and opportunities in its rise to influence in an increasingly uncertain international environment. No major power's foreign policy can be effective without a guiding framework of underlying principles reflecting its geopolitical requirements and values.

ASEAN looks towards India because of its potential as an

economic powerhouse and partly to balance China's overwhelming economic and strategic influence. India should envisage a new strategic architecture for Asia and its own pivotal role in it.

The recent global economic slowdown requires India to diversify its markets. It is imperative that India send out strong positive signals and underline its commitment to be a partner in Asian growth and development.

India's LEP supported India's economic transformation and growth, expanded India's strategic space to pursue its national interests and pursue a proactive role in the in the ongoing process of Asian integration. Regional integration creates an "arc of prosperity", and is reflective of India's desire to see its neighbourhood transform into a "community".

India's objectives in its LEP and visibility in South East Asia can be furthered through areas-education (human resources development), democracy and culture-where it has a comparative advantage over other Asian countries.

India may be a messy democracy, but it has shown a lot of ingenuity in managing a multiracial, multicultural and extremely diverse and complex society. India has tremendous experience in nation building, and conducting fair and peaceful elections periodically. South East Asian nascent democracies have a lot to learn about India's democratic successes.

Higher education is also a very promising area, where India will continue to share her vast expertise with ASEAN countries. Vocational training and training in English language skills of India is much sought after. India has also several advantages in Information Technology (IT), which it can readily share with the region.

Cultural diplomacy also can cement bonds with India's vast civilizational ties with South East Asia. Tourism also can be leveraged to benefit both India and ASEAN. Islamic and Buddhist sites in India are not projected enough in South East Asia. The possibilities are thus immense for India-ASEAN engagement and Cooperation.

Notes

1. A.V.R. Panchamukhi and Rehman Sobhan (Eds) "Towards an Asian Economic Area", *Macmillan,* New Delhi, 1995.
2. Frederic Gare and Amitabh Mattoo (Eds) "India and ASEAN-The Politics of India's Look East Policy", *Manohar Publishers,* New Delhi, 2001.
3. Asian Economic Integration-Vision of a New Asia, *Conference Proceedings, RIS,* Tokyo, November 2004.
4. K.S Nathan, (Eds) India and ASEAN: The Growing Partnership for the Twenty-first Century, *Institute for Diplomacy and Foreign Relations*, Kuala Lumpur, 2000.
5. Friedman Thomas, "The World is Flat", *Allen Pane* (Penguin Books), 2005.
6. Roger Cohen, The Roar of a New Asia is in the Global Horizon, *International Herald Tribune,* April 2005.
7. Sudhir Devare, India and South East Asia-Towards Security Convergence, *ISEAS, Singapore and Capital publishing company,* New Delhi, 2006.
8. Mohammed Ayub, India and South East Asia: Indian Perceptions and Policies-Look East Policy, *Manohar Publishers,* New Delhi, 2001.
9. Rahul Bedi, A new doctrine for the Indian Navy, *Frontline (India),* July 2004.
10. Kanti Bajpai, Enhancing Ties between India and South East Asia: An Indian View, in *India South East Asia and the United States: New opportunities and prospects for co-operation edited by Satu P. Limaye and Ahmed Mukarram, ISEAS,,* Singapore 1998.
11. Ali Alatas, Clash of Civilizations? No it is Pure Evil, *Straits Times*, 16 July, 2004.
12. Jaswant Singh, Defending India, *McMillan India*, Chennai, 1999.
13. K.S Sulu and A. Macaw, Indian Communities in South East Asia: An Indian View, *ISEAS,* Singapore, 1993.

2

India and Australia: Beneficial Bilateralism

2.1 Background

Destination India seems to be the latest buzzword in business circles Down Under. Though India is placed at an "unlucky" 13th position of the total international trade of Australia at present, the Australian Trade Commission feels that the country can well share the first position in a few years' time.

Traditionally, Australian companies have focused on Far-eastern nations like China, Indonesia, Japan, Singapore, Thailand and Korea due to logistical advantage and lower tariffs. But now, the Australian giants have realized India's huge market potential.

As an indicator, Australia's trade with China stands at nearly four times that of India. However, India is now being perceived as the "second" China due to its huge market size. Going by the present trends, it is expected that India will equal China in about five year's time.

The sectors that have attracted attention are minerals, specialized telecom and IT hardware, and processed foods, fruits and vegetables. However, emerging areas include environment management products, medical hardware, health consultancy services, hospital management, tourism, film production and specialized IT software.

Infrastructure sector is another area that is seeing participation of Australian companies. Three Australian companies are participating in Sahara Group's flagship project, Amby Valley, in terms of designing and development.

Similarly, several Indian companies are also vying for the Australian market. Birla and Sterlite have recently bought two mines in Australia. Other sectors attracting Indian corporates include IT, minerals, and steel and steel products. Nearly a US$ 0.87 billion is currently flowing from India to Australia.

The Australian and Indian Governments are dedicated to improving competitiveness and to building greater links between their Economies and regional and global economies. They are also giving a more active role to business. Regulatory burdens that Government has in the past placed upon business are being drastically reduced. These reforms will further strengthen their economies and their bilateral commercial ties.

The private sector has responded strongly to the new environment. These reform processes have put Australia and India in a position where they are very competitive in Asia-Pacific markets. India has recognized that economic dynamism can only be achieved by releasing the energies of the private sector, and by integrating with the world economy. India's influence in East Asia and the broader Asia-Pacific region will only grow in the years ahead. The pattern of trade too has shifted, with India's exports to the Asia-Pacific region far outpacing the growth of exports to any other region.

2.2 Indo-Australian Bilateral Engagement: An Overview

In the post-Pokharan-2 and post-September 11th world, Indo-Australian relations have taken on a new meaning. India's "Look east" and "Extended Neighbourhood" policy initiated in the early 1990s, has acquired new dimensions in Australia. Despite past misgivings, India is being recognized "Down Under" as economically, culturally and politically compatible. The shared "British Commonwealth" legacy of parliamentary democratic pluralism, respect for private property and rule-of –the law, and of course the English language, have brought new economic and strategic complementarities to Indo-Australian relations. Australia's "Look West" policy now goes beyond the ASEAN region to include India in her economic and strategic calculations.

There is growing realisation on both sides to step-up

economic cooperation. A perception perhaps lingers in Canberra that India, could become a rival if India is allowed greater access to the Asia-Pacific region; but the emergence of China as a major economic and strategic player in the region, has tempered Australian misconceptions. India's growing diplomatic clout in the ASEAN, her economic dynamism, rapid modernization and integration with the world economy, will only strengthen Indo-Australian relations.

Thus, from a phase of "benign neglect", the two countries have reached the stage of "realisation of the potential". India is now certainly more than a small "blimp" on Australia's economic and strategic radar screen.

2.3 Indian-Australian Economies: An Update

2.3.1 Indian Economy: Reforming and Globalizing: India has gone through more than a decade of economic reforms. Beginning in 1991, the thrust of reforms was fiscal stabilization, and initiation of major structural reforms aimed at industrial de-regulation and globalization to induce accelerated investment, growth and employment.

The financial sector reforms have been brought into balance with sustainable balance of payments, foreign currency assets at US$ 100 billion, and a comfortable servicing of debt-repayments. Inflation levels are at record lows of less than 5 percent in the last five years, and poverty ratio has fallen from 36 percent in the early 1990s to less than 28 percent in 2004-05. However, there have been major infrastructural bottlenecks-inadequate good-quality roads and lack of serious reforms in the power sector. The Information Technology (IT) sector has also made rapid strides, and India has emerged as a key player in IT and IT-enabled services.

The key disappointment of the 1990s has been inadequate employment generation-with employment elasticities rapidly coming down in the organized sector. There has also been an "absolute" fall in agricultural employment.

Second generation Reforms have already been initiated,

and it is hoped that acceleration in economic growth and exports will follow, without significant changes in the socio-political parameters. India is now focusing on labour-market reforms and disinvestment in the public-sector, besides speeding up the liberalization and globalization process.

2.3.2 Australian Economy: Liberalizing Frontiers: Australia's open free-market economy was further liberalized in 1988, with the federal Governments' financial de-regulation of the economy. Trade rationalization in consonance with APEC (Asia-Pacific Economic Co-operation) guidelines, competition policies, labour market reforms, and accelerating overall competitiveness, are some of the other features of the Australian economy in the new millennium.

The Australian economy has shifted away from dependence on resources (particularly mining) and agriculture-based industries to a wide range of financial and service-oriented industries. The biggest growth areas are IT-development, where Australia, like India is in some areas, well into the forefront of the new-technology age.

Australia's open and efficient regulatory environment, sound legal system for dispute-settlement and contract-enforcement has placed it well to attract foreign investment. She has an increasingly large pool of professionals working in IT, engineering, legal, accounting, and management consulting, gelling well with the old economy sectors of mining, oil and gas and agri-business.

Australia is no longer reliant upon exports of agricultural and mining products. It is now increasingly a source of high-value added manufactures and services. Trade now amounts to fully 40 percent of Australia's GDP-up from 30 percent only ten years ago. Manufactures now total over 30 percent of merchandise exports. Services amount to nearly a quarter of all exports. These reform processes have put Australia in a position, where it is now very competitive in the Asia-Pacific markets.

2.4 Bilateral Trade

Principal Indian **Exports** to Australia are:

- Rotating electrical parts and plants
- Pearls and gems.
- Textiles and clothing.
- Chemicals and related products.
- Engineering products.
- Leather goods.

Principal Indian **Imports** from Australia are:

- Coal ,Coking Coal and Mining equipment
- Gold
- Wool.
- Copper.
- Base metal and ores.
- Diamonds.
- Wheat.
- Software.
- Automotive components and Services.
- Food processing equipment.

2.5 Some Observations on Indo-Australian Trade

1. Indian imports from Australia stood at US$ 11.26 billion in 2008. Primary commodities still dominate Australian exports to India.
2. Among primary products, coal continues to be the major export item, with wool, cotton, legumes, copper ores and processed metals also significant.
3. ETMs (Elaborately Transformed Manufactures) mainly mining, machinery, telecommunications equipment and electrical machinery are becoming increasingly significant.
4. India ranked 4th in Australia's export market with a share of 6.1 % in terms of overall exports
5. On current growth rates, India will be one of Australia's top ten export markets in the next five years.

2.6 Investment-based Co-operation

Australian investment in India covers banking and financial services, manufacturing, telecommunications, hotels, mineral processing, food processing, oil and gas and automotive parts.

Some of the major Australian companies which have presence in India include: Telstra (telecommunications); BHP Billiton (mining); Rio Tinto (mining); MIM Holdings (mining); Snowy Mountains Engineering Corporation (infrastructure development); Argyle diamonds (technical support office for diamond sales); P & O (development of container ports); Orica Limited (joint venture with Imperial Chemical Industries); Lucent Technologies (IT) and ANZ (IT).

2.7 Indo-Aussie Business Ties

The Australian domestic market remains small to medium by world standards, and in many of the industries the success and growth factors are from "exports" or "potential exports". Australian tariff barriers have been considerably lowered, and the objective will be to keep on lowering them, so as to make import-substitution competitive and favourable for business development.

Effort has been made by both Governments and Industry Chambers to increase awareness about potential business opportunities. The scenario has changed recently, as India gets access to international money markets for making overseas investment through ADR/GDR issues.

The match between Indian resources and expertise, with those in Australia will often lead to profitable business ventures.

Tourism and the Hospitality industries have been areas that have witnessed considerable growth, and hold lot of future potential.

Sport, Entertainment and their media links are also areas, which can be strengthened in the years to come.

Australia's leading Fosters beer is now bottled in India, and has been proven successful in many cities.

The Indian entertainment industry, particularly Hindi films, has been a major factor in bringing Australia closer to India. After seeing Indian movies many Indians want to visit Australia, with their projection of Australia's scenic beauty, and particularly the Sydney Opera House. Over thirty Indian movies were shot in Australia and many more are in the pipeline. Australia offers some of the most picturesque shooting spots, and post-production facilities for film shooting.

2.8 Wrap-up

In conclusion, there is growing realisation by both Australia and India to step-up trade, investments, and dialogue. However, some of the problem areas are:

- Australian companies face problems on account of obstinate lower-level Indian bureaucrats, who often renege on unwritten commitments.
- Multifarious clearances are required at various levels stifling any fresh business ideas.
- Australian companies can help India in exploiting its vast mineral resources to India's advantage, as Australia has superior and time-tested expertise in mineral-exploitation.
- Information technology, environment technology, health and tourism are some of the areas where Indo-Aussie collaboration can be intensified.
- Australia also offers excellent and reasonable high-quality higher education compatible with the Indian system. Many Indian students now study in Australian Universities, and the educational flow will only grow in the years to come.
- Inter-State differences in environmental norms of India and the fact that Mining is a State subject also hampers greater Australian investment to India.

Thus sustained bilateral economic engagement and strategic interaction can take Indo-Australian relations to a higher diplomatic plane.

References

Australian websites: www.dfat.gov.au and www.ausgovindia.com.

Barua, Amit; Renewing Indo-Australian Ties; *Frontline*; 13th May 2001, pp. 49-50.

Economic Survey (various issues); Government of India, Ministry of Finance.

India-New Economy, Old Economy, Department of Foreign Affairs and Trade, Commonwealth of Australia, 2001.

Janelle, Bonor, *Australia-India Security Relations: Common Interest or Common Disinterest?* Working Paper, No.67, New South Wales, Australian Defence Studies Centre, April 2001.

Kenneth McPherson, Pai Panandiker and Marika Vicziamy (eds), *Australia and India in the Context of the Indian Ocean and APEC Regions,* Centre for Policy Research, New Delhi, 2000 (Mimeo).

World Bank, *World Development Reports* (various issues).

3

Indo-Malaysian Ties: New Synergies

3.1 Malaysian Economy

Malaysia has raced ahead into the twenty-first century in the age of information technology and e-commerce. The structural transformation of the country's economy over the last thirty years has been spectacular. The national has not rested on its laurels. Because of its wealth of mineral resources and fertile soils, but has taken decisive steps in progressing from an economy dependent on agriculture to an export-driven economy spurred by high technology, knowledge-based and capital-intensive industries.

A market-oriented economy, combined with social and political stability, an educated workforce, and an infrastructure which provides easy access to the rest of the world, has encouraged the private sector in Malaysia to not only flourish but became partners with the public sector in the nation's development. This business-oriented and business-friendly environment has resulted in Malaysia being one of the largest recipients of FDI (Foreign Direct Investment) among developing countries.

Over the last few years, the Malaysian economy achieved an average growth rate between 5-7 percent, with GDP reaching US$ 184 billion in 2007. Exports and imports have more than quadrupled, placing Malaysia among the world's top twenty trading nations.

The regional economic and financial crisis, which hit several countries in the Asia-Pacific in mid-1997 and caused a currency crisis and stock market crash in Malaysia, provided further proof of the strength and resilience of the Malaysian economy. Within less than two years, helped by selective exchange controls and the pegging of the Ringgit, which provided stability to business, Malaysia has bounced back on the track towards economic recovery. However, the global financial crisis of 2008 has hit the economy again.

As per *Malaysian Economy, 4th Quarter Review*, "The Malaysian economy rebounded 4.5% (Q3 2009: -1.2%) after recording three consecutive quarters of negative growth. For the whole of 2009, the economy contracted 1.7% (2008: 4.6%). The strong rebound in the quarter was supported by higher domestic demand and exports. On the supply side, all sectors in the economy recorded positive growth except mining, which declined at a slower rate. After recording four consecutive quarters of negative growth, the manufacturing sector turned around to register a growth of 5.3% (Q3 2009: -8.6%) following significant improvement in global demand for electrical and electronic (E&E) products. The services sector, the largest contributor, expanded further by 5.1% (Q3 2009: 3.4%) led by finance and insurance, real estate and business services as well as communication sub-sectors. The construction sector grew strongly by 9.2% (Q3 2009: 7.9%) largely due to higher activities in the non-residential sub-sectors and special trade works".

The manufacturing sector has continued to be the engine of growth of the Malaysian economy, helped by a steady growth of new investments and re-investments by MNCs as well as local companies. Today Malaysia is among the world's leading exporters not only of products manufactured from her natural resources of rubber, palm oil and timber, but also those in the electrical and electronics sector such as audio and video products, computer hard disk drives, semiconductor devices and room air-conditioners.

The general economic structure of Malaysia is shown in Table 3.1.

The Malaysian economy is likely to continue the process of recovery, and regain its position of pre-eminence as a growing market for imports, and attracting larger foreign investment. The Malaysian market will continue to follow liberal import policies with relatively low tariffs. Thus Malaysia can easily be described as an economy with growing prosperity and expanding size of the market.

Table 3.1: General Economic Structure of Malaysia: Main Economic Indicators, 2009

GDP at current prices (RM billion)	674.43
GNP at current prices (RM billion)	681.00
Per Capita Income (RM)	24,055
Total Exports (RM billion)	553.29
Total Imports (RM billion)	434.94
Gross International Reserves (US$ billion)	96.71

3.2 Malaysian Foreign Trade Structure and Trade Policy

Malaysia's external trade policy has evolved against a background where the external sector has been as important contributor to the country's economic growth. About two-thirds of the country's GDP are from external trade. Being a relatively small country, Malaysia had to venture beyond its borders to market its products and services.

The external sector is an important source of capital, input and technology. The commitment to a multilateral trading system that is predictable and stable is thus imperative for Malaysia's economic prosperity. These factors underline Malaysia's approach to trade-related policy formulation.

Malaysia has, an open and outward oriented trade regime replacing the largely substitution policies of the late 1960s and early 1970s. While seeking better international prospects for its products and services, and access to better inputs, components and technology, Malaysia also accepts responsibilities and obligations commensurate with its level of economic development.

These principles are embodied in Malaysia's trade policy objectives, which are:

- To undertake liberalization measures through regular reviews of the trade regime;
- To maintain and expand Malaysia's trade with major

trading partners;

- To diversify and expand trade in new and emerging markets;
- To promote and develop exports of manufactured and value added resource-based products;
- To seek improved and favourable market access for Malaysia's exports of processed commodities and manufactured products;
- To promote and develop exports of Malaysia's services;
- To strengthen and expand intra-ASEAN trade through closer economic and trade cooperation. Consistent with its liberal and outward-oriented trade policies, Malaysia trades with over 200 countries.

3.3 Indo-Malaysian Trade

Bilateral trade between India and Malaysia dates back to 2000 years and the ancient Hindu kingdoms of the Pal lavas and Cholas actively traded with Malaya. In the fifties and sixties, India's mixed economy and democratic set-up was not only appreciated by the two superpowers, but was also admired by many South East Asian countries, who sought direction from India for their domestic and foreign policies. However, in the 1970s and 1980s, India's economic progress came to be regarded as not only being unsatisfactory and stagnant but also less attractive for economic cooperation. As a result, India's bilateral economic cooperation with ASEAN countries constituted barely 2 percent of the total commercial transactions of the group. The only exception was Malaysia, with which India had traditional ties.

The Indian Government of P.V Narasimha Rao in 1992, which consciously turned *East* forging closer ties with South-East Asia through ASEAN, gave fillip to Indo-Malaysian ties. India became a full-dialogue partner of ASEAN in 1996. India also has consciously attempted to provide an explicit economic orientation to its foreign policy, and the look east policy fits into this strategy. In the present international economic environment, India and Malaysia would gain significantly by increasing trade and economic interaction. India can also use Malaysia as springboard for increasing access to other markets of ASEAN.

3.4 Joint Ventures and Investment-based Co-operation

India's performance on the trade front in Malaysia has been inadequate, but she has been very successful in the performance of industrial ventures set up by the Indian business community in Malaysia. There are about 20 Indians Joint Ventures currently in operation in Malaysia. Malaysian investment in India peaked in1998, but has since been falling. Indian investment Malaysia has been the highest in textiles and synthetics, followed by the engineering and electrical sector and pharmaceuticals and chemicals. Because of the traditional links, there have been investment flows in both directions. They cover palm oil refining, manufacture of drugs and pharmaceuticals, textiles and yarn, automobile associated activities, steel rubber and informatics. India is the fifth largest investors in Malaysia after Japan, US, Taiwan and Singapore. From the Malaysian viewpoint, they are looking for Indian expertise in science and technology, R & D, space technology, software, healthcare and pharmaceuticals. Private sector participation is also taking-off in a big way.

As many as 15 agreements were signed between Indian and Malaysian companies during Prime Minister Vajpayee's visit to Malaysia in May 2001. This should lay the foundation for a more focused trade and business partnership. The agreements include a renewal of collaboration between the Indian Oil Corporation and Petronas, and between HMT and Orion Java, Malaysia to set up a watch assembly plant. An MOU was also signed between CII and the Asian Strategy and Leadership Incorporated (ASLI) to promote bilateral trade and information exchange between the two countries.

The Malaysian side expressed concern on the issue of increased Indian duties on imports of palm oil, which the

Indian Government will be reviewing. Indian firms are also operating in the Multimedia Super Corridor. Malaysia became part of a select group of countries to cooperate with India in space technology through the GSLV. In a bid to correct the trade imbalance (heavily in Malaysia's favour) the Indian Government decided to offer a US$ 50 million credit line for imports of project-related industrial goods into Malaysia from India. Some potential areas for India-Malaysia joint collaboration include electronic products, textiles, shipbuilding and infrastructure development.

3.5 Andhra Pradesh and Malaysia

A joint task force of officials of Andhra Pradesh and Malaysia Governments has been set up to coordinate activities relating to investments, joint ventures and other areas of mutual interest.

The Malaysian Government offered to take up highway projects between Tada and Icchapuram, Hyderabad–Vijayawada, and outer ring road for Hyderabad and showed interest in the new international airport near Hyderabad.

A memorandum of understanding was also signed recently for establishing Hyderabad as a regional Hub for global internet traffic. There is proposal a lay a optical fibre submarine link between Hyderabad- Visakhapatnam and Kuala Lumpur for the development and operation of high bandwidth transmission infrastructure for international data, voice, video and internet communication traffic.

The concept of Andhra Pradesh's Vision 2020 Document has been borrowed from the original Malaysian Government's Vision 2020. Emphasis on Tourism and information Technology by Andhra Pradesh is also influenced by Malaysia's experience.

3.6 Observations on Indo-Malaysian Cooperation

The following observations are made on Indo-Malaysian cooperation:

1. Despite repeated requests, Malaysia has not cleared the application of same Indian banks to set up branches in Kuala Lumpur. Considering the growth in bilateral trade and potential that exists for it, there can be no plausible reason to delay the setting up of Indian banks in both countries. This is considered by both trade and industry as a primary requisite to spur trade.
2. Another thrust sector will be Ports. Malaysia has embarked on a major exercise to modernize its own ports and taken on even Singapore that boasts to be the regional port hub. Malaysian investors are looking for collaborative ventures in Tamil Nadu and A.P. to develop new and minor ports on the coasts.
3. Indian can also provide assistance to Malaysia in Science and technology, R and D, space and Technology, and software for the Multi-Media Super Corridor.
4. In the perception of Malaysians, Indian goods don't match up in quality. Indian companies aren't aggressive enough about selling and they are too pre-occupied with quick profits, rather than building long term relationships.
5. India's strength in Malaysia will lie with providing consultancy services, project management and human resources development perspective—a lot more than mere goods.
6. Over-reliance on partners of Indian origin will not help units to go very far in tapping the potential business opportunities provided by the growing Malaysian markets. Economic power lies in the hands of people of Chinese origin, who also operate on behalf on MNCs from the developed countries including Japan, and control distribution channels.
7. Stagnating (or declining) exports to Malaysia, and increasing imports from Malaysia, has resulted in the trade balance on an average becoming more and more unfavourable to India.
8. The bilateral trade between India and Malaysia still

accounts for very small proportion of each country's trade with the rest of the world. The volume of trade between the two countries is relatively small, and not commensurate with their economic potential.

9. Lack of adequate market information and marketing research on the part of both Indian exporters and Malaysian importers, could be responsible for stagnation of Indian exports to Malaysia.
10. Aggressive marketing by Indian products for their "high quality" manufactured and semi manufactured products in the competitive Malaysian market needs to be done.
11. High tariff and non-tariff barriers prevailing in India compared to levels prevailing in the ASEAN countries.
12. Lack of export culture at micro-level: and of export competitiveness of Indian products (in terms of the package of customer satisfaction comprising dimensions like price, quality, delivery schedules and after sales servicing through physical presence.
13. Lack of sophistication in commercial negotiating skills, among Indian diplomats in embassies in target countries.
14. Bureaucratic hurdles for clearance of investment proposal in transparent and expeditious corruption-free manner.
15. The image of the Indian government as a hesitant reformer under democratic pressures (leading to delays in reforms such as labour market reforms) and as a slow and discriminating implementer of policies already communicated.

4

India and Singapore: Trade and Economic Co-operation

4.1 Introduction

The city-state of Singapore is strategically located at a critical intersection of international commerce, and in the geo-strategic vicinity of India and China. Singapore commands attention on the international stage as a dynamic economy, and according to Michael Leifer as an "exceptional state".

India's links with Southeast Asia go back centuries. India has left the imprint of its great civilization all over the region-in religion, culture, arts and literature. However, during the first four decades after India's independence, India turned inwards. Its priority was self-sufficiency rather than interdependence, and these historic linkages weakened. Today, India is once again opening up and rediscovering the region. It is attracting investments from all over the world, especially in IT (Information Technology). Outward investments from India have also been increasing. Its external trade has increased, and with Southeast Asia trade has multiplied six times in the last ten years. If the reforms continue, India's interests and influence in the region will continue to grow. India's "Look East" policy and economic liberalization efforts coincided with Singapore's regionalization strategy of investing in emerging economies, providing a common ground for cooperation. Singapore is a natural gateway for India to engage in the region, because of its historical ties and special friendship between the two countries.

There have been many high-level visits exchanged between the two countries, including Heads of State and Heads of Government visits. Bilateral agreements on avoidance of double taxation, cooperation in shipping, tourism, civil aviation, information technology and science and technology have been signed between India and Singapore.

Singapore also played a leading role in India becoming a member of the ARF (ASEAN Regional Forum) and the ASEAN+1 Summit. Among the ASEAN states Singapore has gone the farthest to improve both bilateral and Associational ties. India's former Prime Minister, P.V Narasimha Rao, in his path-breaking Singapore lecture of September 1994, which set in motion India's "Look East Policy". The Asia-Pacific could be the spring board for our leap into the global market place. I am happy to have had this opportunity to enunciate my belief in this vision of a new relationship between India and the Asia-Pacific from Singapore, which I consider the geographic and symbolic centre of the Asia-Pacific". Since then, Singapore has been the key country for India's engagement with Southeast Asia. It was the country coordinator for the ASEAN-India dialogue. Singapore's exertions on behalf of India are openly acknowledged by the Indian policy making community.

During his visit to Singapore in August 2003, the then Indian External Affairs Minister candidly noted: "... in the development of our ties with ASEAN, few countries have been as creative and pro-active as Singapore. We are grateful to our many friends here, in particular, (then) Prime Minister Goh Chok Tong, for his vision and leadership in bringing India and ASEAN closer.

This has been made possible by virtue of the strong bilateral relationship that India and Singapore have built over the years". Prime Minister Lee Hsien Loong, in a recent speech in New Delhi in July 2005, noted: "... India's influence is being felt all over Southeast Asia. In Singapore alone, there are more than 1,500 Indian companies. Many are regional headquarters, some even overseeing operations in the Indian market. Thousands of Indian professionals work in Singapore in IT, financial services and other fields. Bollywood movies enjoy a strong following ...the stage has been set for a burgeoning bilateral relationship between Singapore and India, and wider and deeper cooperation between India and Southeast Asia. With greater collaboration and integration between the people of both sides, and continued reforms by those in Government, we can look forward to a vibrant and dynamic future for Asia".

The increasingly close relations between India and Singapore in recent years have been underpinned by a dramatic growth in bilateral trade and investment links. The major items of Indian exports to Singapore are textile manufactures including apparel and yarn, precious stones and pearls, parts for office and data machines, aluminium, electrical machinery, fish and fish products and fruits and vegetables. The major items of India's imports from Singapore have been petroleum products, machinery, metallic ores/scrap, organic chemicals, primary plastics and scientific instruments. Singapore's economy complements India's economy, and does not threaten India's sensitive sectors. Singapore-India trade stood at S$ 10.285 billion during the period January-April 2008. Singapore is India's largest trading and investment partner in ASEAN and can therefore, play a useful role as a pathfinder for India.

The Comprehensive Economic Cooperation Agreement (CECA) signed between India and Singapore in June 2005, created the necessary conducive environment for a strong bilateral relationship, and wider cooperation between India and Southeast Asia. CECA combines liberalized commercial transactions in goods and services, with two-way investment flows in untapped areas. It is a very big psychological step for India, signifying a new direction in India's economic diplomacy. It is India's first overarching economic pact with any country. Integral to the CECA is a wide array of established practices and proposed initiatives, ranging from dispute settlement arrangements and a review mechanism to an updated avoidance of double-taxation and other measures. India through the CECA has moved from the old policy of substantial self sufficiency to one where it wants to link up and open up markets in a controlled sort of way, and encourage linkages and exchanges. The CECA lays the groundwork for agreements with many other countries.

With an investment of US$ 2.37 billion during 2009-10, Singapore has emerged as the second largest foreign investor in the country. The major investments in India from Singapore are channelised through three major agencies, viz. Government of Singapore Investment Corporation, Monetary Authority of Singapore and Temasak Holdings. Many Indian companies, mainly trading and software companies have set up joint ventures and subsidiaries in Singapore to promote their business activities in the region, covering diverse product areas such as automobile ancillaries, precision tooling, palm kernel processing, micro and mini computers.

In the tourism sector, opportunities are emerging rapidly for Singapore as Indian tourists have become the highest spenders among the tourists to Singapore, and the fourth largest revenue generating market, with growing affluence among the Indian middle class. In the logistics sector, the Port of Singapore Authority (PSA) has been involved in port development and management in Tuticorin in Tamil Nadu and Piparav in Gujarat. These developments have the potential to lead to major investment opportunities for other Singapore firms in the logistics sector.

Defence-related research could be an area of future cooperation. Incremental interactions have taken place across a wide spectrum, ranging from education and culture. Singapore is also keen that India plays an appropriate role in a "creative fashion" in the maintenance of security along the Straits of Malacca.

4.2 Singapore Economy

A former colonial trading port, serving the regional economies of maritime Southeast Asia, Singapore aspired to be a "global city" serving world markets and major multinational corporations. A quarter century after Independence in 1965, the city-state had become a manufacturing centre with one of the highest incomes in the region. As one of Asia's four "little dragons" or newly industrializing economies, Singapore along with the Republic of Korea (South Korea), Taiwan, and Hong Kong was characterized by an export-oriented economy, relatively equitable income distribution, trade surpluses with the United States and other developed countries, and a common heritage of Chinese civilization and Confucian values. The small island had no resources other than its strategic location and the skills of its nearly 2.7 million people. It has claimed a set of economic superlatives in the 1980s, including the world's busiest port, the world's highest rate of annual economic growth (11 percent), and the world's highest savings rate (42 percent of income).

Singapore has lived by international trade, as it had since its founding in 1819, and operated as a free port with free markets. Its small population and dependence on international markets meant that regional and world markets were larger than domestic markets, which presented both business managers and government policymakers with distinctive economic challenges and opportunities. The value of Singapore's international trade was more than three times its gross domestic product (GDP). The country's year-to-year economic performance fluctuated unpredictably with the cycles of world markets, which were beyond the control or even the influence of Singapore's leaders. In periods of growing international trade, such as the 1970s, Singapore could reap great gains, but even relatively minor downturns in world trade could produce deep recession in the Singapore economy, as happened in 1985-86. The country's dependence on and vulnerability to international markets shaped the economic strategies of Singapore's leaders.

The economy rests on five major sectors: the regional entrepôt trade; export-oriented manufacturing; petroleum refining and shipping; production of goods and services for the domestic economy; and the provision of specialized services for the international market, such as banking and finance, telecommunications, and tourism. The spectacular growth of manufacturing in the 1970s and 1980s had a major impact on the economy and the society, but tended to obscure what carried over from the economic structure of the past. Singapore's economy always depended on international trade and on the sale of services. An entrepôt was essentially a provider of services such as wholesaling, warehousing, sorting and processing, credit, currency exchange, risk management, ship repair and provisioning, business information, and the adjudication of commercial disputes. In this perspective, which focused on exchange and processing, the 1980s assembly of electronic components and manufacture of precision optical instruments were evolutionary steps from the nineteenth century sorting and grading of pepper and rubber. Both processes used the skills of Singaporeans to add value to commodities that were produced elsewhere and destined for consumption outside the city-state.

The dependence on external markets and suppliers pushed Singapore toward economic openness, free trade, and free markets. In the 1980s, Singapore was a free port with only a few revenue tariffs and a small set of protective tariffs scheduled for abolition in the 1990s. It had no foreign exchange controls or domestic price controls. There were no controls on private enterprise or investment, nor any limitations on profit remittance or repatriation of capital.

Foreign corporations were welcome, foreign investment was solicited, and fully 70 percent of the investment in manufacturing was foreign. The government provided foreign and domestic enterprises with a high-quality infrastructure, efficient and graft-free administration, and a sympathetic concern for the problems of businesses.

The vulnerability inherent in heavy dependence on outside markets impelled Singapore's leaders to buffer their country's response to perturbations in world markets and to take advantage of their country's ability to respond to changing economic conditions. Unable to control so much that affected their nation's prosperity, they concentrated on those domestic institutions that could be controlled. The consequence was an economy characterized by a seemingly paradoxical adherence to free trade and free markets in combination with a dominant government role in macroeconomic management and government control of major factors of production such as land, labour, and capital. The extraordinarily high domestic savings rate provided reserves to weather such economic storms as trade recessions and generated a pool of domestically controlled capital that could be invested to serve the long-term interests of Singapore rather than of foreign corporations.

The high savings rate, however, was the result of carefully formulated government programs, which included a compulsory contribution of up to 25 percent of all salaries to a government-controlled pension fund. The government held about 75 percent of the country's land, was the largest single employer, controlled the level of wages, and housed about 88 percent of the population in largely self-owned apartments. It also operated a set of wholly-owned government enterprises and held stock in additional domestic and foreign firms. Government leaders, deeply aware of Singapore's need to sell its services in a competitive international market, continually stressed the necessity for the citizens to master high levels of skills and to subordinate their personal wishes to the good of the community. The combination of devotion to free-market principles and the need for internal control and discipline in order to adapt to the demands of markets reminded observers of many family firms, and residents of the country commonly referred to it as Singapore Inc.

With a limited domestic market and almost no natural resources, Singapore was forced to integrate into the global economy early in its development. When Singapore separated from Malaysia, it lost its hinterland. It had no choice but to swiftly shift to an export-driven industrialization policy, slashing trade barriers and actively seeking foreign investment. This change in orientation brought Singapore an average growth rate of 10 percent from 1965 to 1979. In 1965, when Singapore first became independent, its total trade amounted to US$ 6.8 billion.

For the year 2009, Singapore's total merchandise trade stood at S$747 billion, a decline of 19 percent compared to 2008. This decline in total trade was the largest since records started in 1964, and it brought the level of total trade in 2009 below that of 2006.

Singapore has grown from a third world country, and the continued rapid economic development over the past years owes much to its open trade regime, clearly directed economic management and its position in the centre of a dynamic regional market.

Political stability and a well developed infrastructure combine with very high rates of savings and investment, and attractive investment incentives have contributed to make the economy one of the strongest in the world.

Singapore has a highly industrialized economy. Agriculture and mining are of little importance. Their contribution to GDP is close to zero. 90 percent of food consumed in Singapore is imported.

Financial and business services and manufacturing are the most important sectors. The most important manufacturing sector is electronics directly accounting for 52.5 percent of manufacturing export.

By tapping into the global grid of trade, investments, and capital, Singapore recorded an average annual growth rate of 7.3 percent and the nominal value of its non-oil domestic exports have grown by an average of 12 percent per annum. Singapore's trade to GDP ratio is the highest in the world.

The importance of trade to Singapore is illustrated by the fact that since 1999, Singapore's total trade in goods and services has accounted on average for nearly 360 percent of GDP. Singapore is thus an advocate of the multilateral trading system as free trade has been crucial for its survival.

4.3 Trade Performance and Policy Options

Singapore's external trade pattern reflects the conditions in the external environment. Total trade recovered in 1999 as external conditions improved after the Asian financial crisis. Following a 22.9 percent expansion in 2000, Singapore's external trade contracted sharply by 9.4 percent during the 2001 Recession.

It has, however, stayed positive since 2002, with a 9.6 percent expansion in 2003, and an exceptionally strong growth of 22.5 percent in 2004, largely due to the rebound in global electronics demand, increase in pharmaceutical exports and pick up in demand from key markets. Malaysia, the US, EU, Japan, and China were Singapore's top five trading partners, accounting for 59 percent of total trade in 2004.

However, exports and imports decreased by 18 per cent and 21 per cent respectively in 2009 due to the global financial crisis. Singapore's main exports and imports are electronics, oil and chemicals.

Singapore's total trade in services has increased steadily during the past few years. Its major trading partners in trade in commercial services are the US, EU, Japan, and the regional developing economies. The top ten trading partners accounted for more than three-fourths of Singapore's trade in services in 2003. The geographical pattern of Singapore's trade in services is thus broadly similar to trade in goods.

Singapore's export of services can be broadly divided into traditional transportation and travel services and the emerging trade-related financial, business, and technical services. The two most important components of services imports were transportation and travel. Imports of services recorded an annual growth of 11 percent during 1998-2002, though it slowed down during the 2001-03 period amidst a deteriorating labour market, high retrenchments, and the occurrence of SARS.

Singapore's trade policy directions are underpinned by

several factors:

- Constraints of a small domestic market with limited natural resources.
- Its dependence on the global economy; Singapore's economy is plugged into the international grid and cannot be insulated from key global trends. It is vulnerable to developments around the world.
- Its dependence on free access to markets around the world for its economic survival and growth.

The stated objectives of Singapore's trade policies are: to contribute towards the strengthening of a free, open and stable multilateral trading system; to develop Singapore into an international trading centre; to identify new markets while maintaining existing markets; to safeguard and diversify sources of imports; and to increase services exports.

In general, Singapore maintains one of the most liberal trading regimes in the world. It has very few trade barriers and provides a favourable climate for trade cooperation for countries both in the immediate vicinity and beyond. It primarily follows a free trade policy.

Singapore's prosperity is thus inextricably linked to that of the region and the world. To secure and expand its political and economic space, Singapore has adopted a multi-pronged approach in pursuing trade liberalization initiatives through the multilateral trading system, bilateral free trade agreements (FTAs), regional trading arrangements (RTAs), and through regional groupings such as ASEAN, APEC, and ASEM (Asia-Europe Meeting).

Singapore needs to ensure that it remains integrated with the rest of the world through deeper multilateral, regional, and bilateral links. In light of these challenges, Singapore's policy is to continue to promote greater integration at the multilateral, regional, and bilateral levels. It will continue to adopt a multi-pronged approach to trade policy by engaging in bilateral and regional FTA negotiations. It will continue to play a proactive role at the WTO to keep the momentum of multilateral trade liberalization.

4.4 Investment Climate and Policies

Singapore is located at the heart of Southeast Asia which is a resource rich region with a market potential of some 300 million people. Thus, Singapore is well placed to serve the fast growing markets of this region. Singapore's unique location and sophisticated telecommunications network allow financial institutions and other companies in the country to transact business with any part of the world within the same working day.

Singapore has first-class infrastructure in telecommunications and transport particularly in sea and air. Singapore's Changi Airport has the most air-links in the Asia-Pacific.

Singapore has seven Free Trade Zones (FTZs), six for sea-borne cargo and one for air cargo within which a wide range of facilities and services are provided for storage and re-export of dutiable and controlled goods. Goods can be stored within the zones without any customs documentation until they are released in the market. They can also be processed and re-exported with minimum customs formalities. The FTZs at the port facilitate entrepot trade and promote the handling of transshipment cargo. They offer free 72-hour storage for import/re-export cargo.

The Economic Development Board (EDB) promotes foreign investments with a border-less view beyond Singapore and into the region. As Singapore's investment architect, it helps foreign as well as local companies plan global business strategies and configure their activities from their base in Singapore. The EDB adds value to investors by providing a one-stop investment promotion service to identify business opportunities in Singapore and the region, and helps them set up their operations speedily.

Singapore's regulatory environment is business-friendly and is characterized by transparency and clarity. The bureaucracy is generally considered to be efficient and effective. Prior to implementing any law or regulation, the government usually consults relevant bodies and agencies, companies and the public. Various rules and regulations relating to tax, labour, banking, finance, industrial health and safety, arbitration, wages and training are formulated and reviewed with the interests of foreign investors and local enterprises in mind. However, local laws give regulatory bodies, wide discretion to modify and impose new conditions. This allows government agencies to negotiate the way they provide incentives or other services to foreign companies on a case-by-case basis.

Singapore has a highly open investment regime, through which it seeks to overcome land and labour constraints. It aims to progress into the league of developed countries by attracting firms that can build up the country's technological base and labour force capabilities. Moreover, attracting foreign investment into the country has been an economic strategy of the government since independence. Consequently, the country's legal framework and public policies have always been investor-friendly.

The government of Singapore generally does not restrict or discourage foreign investment either to protect local industries or for any other reasons. However, restrictions on investment in a limited number of sectors exist. Armament manufacturing is strictly closed to foreign investment. Other sectors where foreign investments are limited include news media, telecommunications, broadcasting and domestic banking. Moreover; there can be no foreign ownership of public utility services.

Incentives are used both for the promotion of new investments in industries and services and for encouraging existing companies to upgrade through mechanization and automation and through the introduction of new products and services.

4.5 India-Singapore Trade Relations

Singapore is the largest market in ASEAN for India's merchandise exports, followed by Malaysia, Thailand, Indonesia, and the Philippines. Singapore is India's largest trading and investment partners in ASEAN accounting for 38% of Indis's overall trade with ASEAN in 2006. The increasingly close relations between India and Singapore in recent years have been underpinned by a dramatic growth in bilateral trade and investment linkages. India is looking for infrastructure investments, critical technologies and export markets. Singapore has surplus capital and could be a useful partner in infrastructure development in India as well as investment in Indian companies.

The major items of India's exports to Singapore include crude petroleum, refined motor spirit, petroleum oils, polished diamonds for jewellery, polished industrial diamonds, articles of jewellery, aluminum unwrought, aluminium sheets, parts and accessories of computers, synthetic fabrics, silk fabrics, embroidery/table linen of man-made fibres, combed cotton, knitted T-shirts, vests, benzene, dyes, acids, insecticides, fungicides, household articles of stainless steel, corrugated products of iron and steel, forged/stamped articles of iron and steel, bars and rods of iron steel, parts of boring or sinking machinery, X-ray tubes, medical, surgical, dental and veterinary instruments/appliances, penicillin, rice, sugar, cashew nuts, essential oil, crabs live/dried, fish (fresh/chilled/dried), titanium ore, menthol, diesel/semi-diesel generating sets, static converters, valves/taps cocks for pipes, boilers, tanks etc, bus/lorry tyres, tobacco etc. These items in value terms constitute over 70 percent of India's exports to Singapore.

The major items of India's imports from Singapore in constitute parts and accessories of computers and computer peripherals, integrated circuits, cellular phones, CD-ROMs, styrene, P-xylene, O-xylene, polypropylene, vinyl acetate, topped crudes, and parts of boring and sinking machinery.

Nickel, tin (unwrought), lead (unwrought), aluminium (unwrought), zinc (unwrought), waste and scrap of iron and steel, photographic chemicals, sewing machines, ball/roller bearings, parts for bulldozers, parts of aero planes/helicopters, parts for audio/video recorders, medical instruments and appliances, parts of cellular phones, parts of motor vehicles, cigarettes, pigments, parts of cathode ray tubes, auto parts, parts for electrical machines and apparatus. These items in value terms constitute over 60 percent of India's imports from Singapore.

4.6 Investment Patterns

Singapore has emerged amongst the top foreign investors in India. Some of the Government-Linked Corporations (GLCs) of Singapore's projects include Ascendas' Information Technology Park in Bangalore, the participation of the Port of Singapore Authority (PSA) in both equity (40 percent) and management of Piparav Port, Gujarat, PSA's 30-year contract for operation and management of the Tuticorin Port, Singtel's joint venture with Bharati Telecom and Singapore Technologies Telemedia's JV with ModiCorp. The Government of Singapore Investment Corporation (GIC) has registered itself in India as a Financial Institutional Investors, and has committed Rs. 119 million in HDFC Ltd. Apart from investing in other stocks and equities.

Singapore-based MNCs and Singapore's government-linked-companies (GLCs) such as Singapore Telecom, Port of Singapore Authority and Singapore Technologies have also made investments in India. Singapore's private sector companies have made small-scale investments in health care, real estate, and tourism. Favourable experience and profitability of Singapore's technology park in Bangalore has created a positive environment for investments by Singapore in India.

Singapore, through its government holding company, government of Singapore Investment Corporation (SGIC), is also one of the largest Foreign Institutional Investors in India.

The majority of the MNCs in Singapore have used Mauritius to route investments to India because of its favourable double taxation treaty with India. Thus, the official figures of inflows of FDI from Singapore to India are understated, as they exclude those investments routed via Mauritius.

Temasek and Stanchart Bank formed the Merlion-India Fund of US$ 100 million for investing in mid to late stage Indian Companies. The fund does not cover investment in infra - structure, real estate and trading. This fund was set up for the purpose of Singapore companies investing in Indian companies expanding in India and abroad.

The Singapore Business Federation (SBF), which is the government-guided amalgamation of different chambers of commerce and industry, is also likely to open an office in India. Individual chambers of commerce associated with SBF such as the Chinese, Malay and Indian chambers might also open their own separate offices.

While Singapore's manufacturing base cantering on electronics and petrochemicals, and its role as an entrepot centre will continue to sustain the merchandise trade, the emerging opportunities are largely in the services sector, particularly in the Information and Communication Technology (ICT), logistics services, business and financial services, tourism, and health services This is more so as Singapore plans to develop itself into a service hub and improve its capabilities in areas where there exist considerable complementarities with India. The opportunities are not only in trade in services transactions (such as used by Singapore Airlines of India as a base for some of its IT-enabled services) but also in investments (presence of Indian ICT, Pharmaceutical, and trading companies in Singapore, and Singapore's investments in India's ICT, tourism and health services, besides in port development and logistics). The probable involvement of Singapore's polytechnics in technical education in Tamil Nadu, and perhaps other states, could further strengthen bilateral linkages.

The Info-Comm. Development Authority of Singapore (IDA) has signed an MoU with India's premier IT training company, National Institute of Information Technology (NIIT) to persuade IT professionals to locate in Singapore, from anywhere in the world. As Indian professionals are internationally competitive and culturally compatible, India is among the largest sources of IT manpower in the world, a significant proportion is likely to be sourced from India. This could create a dynamic Indian Diaspora with positive externalities for both countries. The investments by Singapore Telecom (SingTel) in India's telecom sector in partnership with India's Bharti Televentures to take advantage of India's huge potential domestic telecom and Internet market is also another example in this sector.

In the tourism sector, opportunities are emerging rapidly for Singapore as Indian tourists have become the highest spenders among tourists to Singapore and became the fourth largest revenue generating market, with growing affluence among the Indian middle class. Singapore tourism authorities has also been actively involved in promoting select areas in India as a tourism destination for Singaporeans, through a joint marketing by the Government of India tourism office already established in Singapore.

Indeed, Singapore's two airlines, Singapore Airlines and Silk Air have quite liberal rights to fly to several destinations in India. They could however take greater advantage of India's open sky policies concerning air cargo. In the logistics sector, the Port of Singapore Authority (PSA) has been involved in port development and management in Tuticorin in Tamil Nadu and Piparav in Gujarat. These have the potential to lead to major investment opportunities for other Singapore firms in the logistics sector. Negotiations between Singapore's largest supermarket operator, NTUC Fairprice which has close links with the government, and India's Apollo Group, one of Asia's largest hospital and health-care management companies to set up a pharmacy and retail chain of convenience stores numbering in the hundreds in petrol stations run by the Indian oil corporation also hold promise for greater economic linkages. It would contribute to Singapore's food security, and to its supply chain for other essential household goods. Indian IT companies have recognized the importance of Singapore as a marketing and development centre, and their presence is growing. As Indian businesses have been given much greater freedom to invest abroad, presence of Indian companies from other sectors in Singapore is also increasing. This should also have a positive impact on Singapore's importance as a business hub, and on trade in business services.

Singapore intends to increasingly rely at the margin on investment income from abroad. Its rather large foreign currency reserves, estimated to be about US$ 198.69 billion in March 2010, are mostly invested abroad through holding companies of the Singapore government. It is suggested that these holding companies consider passive investments in infrastructure projects in India. Setting up of a physical presence in India by the Singapore Government Investment Corporation (SGIC), and other such Singapore government investment companies, merits serious consideration. Currently, these holding companies do act in a limited way as venture capitalists for Indian IT companies. However, there is much greater scope in not only the IT sector but also in biotechnology, life sciences, and other areas. For these purposes also, physical presence in India would be beneficial.

4.7 India-Singapore Comprehensive Economic Cooperation Agreement (CECA): Key Provisions

On June 29, 2005, India and Singapore signed a Comprehensive Economic Co-operation Agreement (CECA), the first of its kind for India, concluding two years of intensive negotiations. Its distinctive feature is that it is indeed 'comprehensive' and covers trade in goods and services, investment flows and encompasses a double taxation avoidance agreement (DTAA). Such wide-ranging agreements are, in a sense, the logical next step in a world economy increasingly driven by the flows of trade in goods, services and movement of capital.

For, India, it seems, the gains driving the partnership with Singapore would be in the area of services exports and in-bound FDI. Singapore accounted for approximately 2.5 percent of India's FDI inflows from 1991 to 2005 and has been investing especially in Indian infrastructure industries such as ports, telecommunications and banks, in the last few years. The Singapore government has in the past indicated its willingness to set up a US$ 1 billion fund to invest in India after the CECA comes into force. Since the island-nation is a free-trading port, most of the duties on its tariff lines are zero and there is much it can offer by way of tariff concessions, though the hope is that synergies in Indian manufacturing and Singaporean branding expertise can be tapped to profit in the ASEAN market. One of the difficult aspects of the negotiations was determining the rules of origin (ROO)-by which the nationality of goods are determined to ensure that only citizens of the contracting country avail of trade concessions-as there were concerns in India that exporters from third countries could use the Singapore route to dump cheap goods inn the country.

The Prime Minister of Singapore, Lee Hsien Loong, believes that the main advantage for Singapore from the agreement is tariff less access to the Indian market in a large number of goods. Besides some banks will have access to the Indian market. For the Indian side, the big gain from the agreement is on the movement of professionals. Also, inward investment into India from Singapore has become very attractive.

The CECA with Singapore is "a free trade agreement (FTA) plus", covers trade in goods as also services, besides investment flows and "mutual recognition" clauses, is expected to help Singapore widen its frontiers of international commerce. Singapore has close economic linkages with the

US, Japan and China among others.

The business communities in both countries could now "leverage" on this win-win development.

In the services sector, Indian companies stand to benefit through increased market access in distribution services, including retail trading, business services, market research, legal, environmental management, management consultancy, tourism, real estate, consultancy and advertising, engineering, architecture and computer-related services.

India is Singapore's 10th largest trading partner with a growing share of 1.87 % in 2004, 2.32 % in 2005, 2.46 % in 2006, 2.80% in 2007 and during the period January-April 2008, Singapore's total trade with India stood at S$ 10.285 billion constituting 3.31 % of Singapore's total world trade (S$ 311 billion).

The provisions of the CECA are broad, aiming not only to liberalise bilateral trade in goods and services but also to increase investment and ease visa regulations. The CECA is likely to enhance further Singapore's position as Asia's trade hub, boost Indian trade with East Asia, and encourage more foreign investment in India.

Under the provisions of the CECA, Singapore will cut all duties on goods made in India (excepting tobacco and automobiles), while India will remove or reduce duties on a range of Singaporean products, covering around four-fifths of its exports.

As a first step India will scrap duties on 506 items immediately (from August 1st) and will phase out tariffs on a further 2,202 items over the next four years, also reducing duties on another 2,407 items by 2009. However, it will maintain the current level of duties on a list of 6,551 items from Singapore. The deal also includes agreements on trade in services and a commitment to liberalise visa requirements for professionals in 127 fields.

4.7.1 Investment Implications: The provisions of the CECA related to investment are equally as significant for

India. During the year 2009-10, Singapore had invested US$ 2.37 billion in India, making it the second-largest investor in the country. (According to the Indian commerce ministry, Singapore's foreign investment in India grew by a whopping 1580 percent during the period 2002-03 to 2009-10 from US$ 150 million to US$ 2370 million.) The CECA has boosted this considerably. Singaporean institutional investments in Indian technology, manufacturing, financial services and aviation were to the tune of US$ 5 billion within the first year of the CECA's implementation, while Singaporean investment in India's infrastructure topped US$ 2 billion.

Certainly, there are measures in the deal that will promote investment. For example, it revamps a bilateral double-taxation-avoidance treaty that was first signed in 1994 to give Singapore the same status as Mauritius (which had hitherto been unique in that its companies could invest in India without paying capital gains tax on profits earned there). The CECA provisions liberalising trade in financial and other services--paving the way for an air-services deal and an open-skies agreement, for example-are also likely to boost business between the two.

The CECA contains some important specific provisions regarding Singaporean investment. It allows the government-linked investment agencies Temasek Holdings and the Government of Singapore Investment Corp each to invest 10 percent stakes in Indian companies, whereas previously they had been restricted to acquiring 10 percent between them. Temasek alone has invested almost US$1.5bn in India, with stakes in India's largest bank (ICICI), its largest healthcare firm (Apollo Hospitals Enterprises), Tata Consultancy Services, and an automotive firm, Mahindra & Mahindra. It is also one of India's foremost private equity investors.

The CECA also opens up India's financial services sector to Singaporean investment, allowing three banks from the city-state--DBS Holdings, Overseas-Chinese Banking Corp and United Overseas Banking to set up branch operations in India.

The three may either set up wholly owned subsidiaries (in which case they will be subject to local regulations) or set up regional branches, in which case they will be limited to opening

4.7.2 Avoidance of Double Taxation Agreement: Double Taxation Agreement (DTA) provides for avoidance of double taxation of income earned in one Contracting State by a resident of the other and makes clear the taxing rights between the two Contracting States on all forms of income from cross-border economic activities between the two Contracting States.

The DTA thus helps to facilitate the flow of trade, investment, technical know-how and expertise between the two Contracting States by eliminating double taxation of income.

Singapore and India have agreed on a protocol to improve the existing DTA, which was signed in January 1994. The main improvement to the DTA is that tax residents will enjoy capital gains tax exemption on investments in India.

However, a tax resident will not be entitled to the capital gains exemption if its affairs are arranged primarily to take advantage of the benefits of the DTA. In addition, a shell/conduit company with negligible or nil business operations or with no real and continuous business activities in Singapore is disallowed from enjoying the capital gains exemption.

For the purposes of the capital gains tax exemption, a company is not a shell company if:

- It is listed on recognised stock exchanges of the Contracting State.
- Its total annual expenditure on operations in the Residence State is equal to or more than S$ 200,000 or Indian Rs. 50, 00,000 in the respective Contracting State as the case may be, in the immediately preceding period of 24 months from the date the gains arise.

The capital gains tax exemption regime of a country is an important consideration for investors and this exemption, which was previously only available to Mauritius, will help promote greater investment flows between Singapore and India.

4.7.3 Trade in Goods: The Trade in Goods Chapter provides for tariff concessions that will make Singapore goods more competitive vis-à-vis other foreign imports into India. Tariffs on approximately 75 percent of Singapore's domestic exports will be eliminated or substantially reduced within 5 years. The sectors benefiting includes electrical and electronics, instrumentation, pharmaceuticals, and plastics.

For Singaporean goods entering India, those that qualify for tariff concessions are classified into one of the following categories: immediate elimination, phased elimination and phased reduction. Goods in the immediate elimination category will have tariffs on them eliminated completely when CECA comes into effect. For goods in the phased elimination and phased reduction categories, the reduction to the final tariffs will be phased in over 5 years and the percentage reduction is expressed as a margin of preference over the Most Favoured Nation (MFN) applied rates.

For Indian goods entering Singapore, Singapore has committed to grant zero-tariff treatment on all imports from India as of entry into force of the Agreement. For example, tariffs on Indian beer entering Singapore will be eliminated.

4.7.4 Rules of Origin: Rules of Origin (ROO) identify the "nationality" of a good. They ensure that only Singaporean or Indian goods enjoy the tariff concessions under CECA.

The general rule of origin is a combination of 40 percent local content and a change in tariff classification at the 4-digit level. CECA also take into consideration the unique production pattern of Singapore and provides for a list of products that are exempt from the general rule. For each of these products, a specific rule of origin (e.g., change in tariff classification only) has been crafted.

4.7.5 Customs: Good customs procedures are necessary to ensure the free movement of goods traded between both countries. The lack of such procedures can increase compliance costs and diminish the benefits that result from tariff reduction.

Under CECA, the customs authorities from India and Singapore will:

- Provide an advance ruling on the eligibility of originating goods for preferential tariffs and tariff classification, upon the request of the trader. This will provide traders with greater certainty on the status of their goods at the country of import.
- Enhance the application of risk management to focus on high-risk goods and facilitate the clearance of low risk consignments. Both authorities will also enhance transparency in regulations so that traders would be fully aware of the requirements and procedures in the respective countries.

4.7.6 Standards and Technical Regulations, Sanitary and Phytosanitary Measures: CECA provides a framework for concluding Mutual Recognition Agreements (MRAs) to eliminate duplicative testing and certification of products to facilitate entry of goods for sale in the respective markets. These sectoral MRAs serve to reduce costs and shorten time to market especially useful for products with short life cycle.

Two sectoral annexes for trade in electrical and electronic products, and telecommunication equipment were concluded under the framework chapter. For products in these two sectors, testing and certification to Indian standards and technical regulations can be done at source. They do not have to be further tested or re-certified on arrival in the market.

The potential benefits are reduction in cost due to elimination of duplicative testing and reduction in time to market for these products to enter the Indian or Singapore market. As most of these products have relatively short life cycles, the result is a reduction in relative cost and improved time to-market competitiveness of Singapore certified products entering the Indian market and vice versa. India is expected to make the necessary amendments to its legislation to implement these MRA arrangements. This may take another 12-18 months. Singapore will also be providing technical training for Indian standards bodies so as to enable them to implement the MRA.

Of immediate benefit is the food sectoral annex where Singapore has facilitated the import of egg products, dairy products and packaged drinking water from India. This will widen the sources of supply for these food products in Singapore.

4.7.7 Investment: The investment chapter aims to promote and protect investments from both countries. Market access for investments is based on the principle of National Treatment subject to the commitments or reservations undertaken. The chapter contains a number of useful features to protect investments. The key features are highlighted as follows:

- *Beneficiaries*: Citizens and Enterprises based in Singapore or India. Indian investors are not required to seek foreign investment approval for coverage under the investment chapter.
- *Broad Range of Investment Instruments*: The chapter covers a broad range of investment instruments and assets, such as equity and debt instruments, Intellectual Property Rights (IPR) and, business licenses and permits. Investments in the nature of both Foreign Direct Investment (FDI) and portfolio investments are covered.
- *National Treatment*: The chapter accords National Treatment to investors from both countries. The market access feature of this provision is subject to the commitments and reservations undertaken.
- *Expropriation and Compensation*: Both countries cannot expropriate investments, directly or indirectly, without proper legal safeguards. Expropriation must be premised on public purpose and compensation based on market value. Land expropriation will be governed by the

domestic legislation of each country.

- *Investor to State dispute settlement*: To give investors greater confidence in investing in either country, both countries have committed to allowing investors, once the investment is established, to take a dispute relating to an obligation under the chapter to an international arbitration tribunal.
- *Free Transfers*: Both countries will allow the investors to freely transfer funds related to their investments, such as capital, profits, dividends and royalties.
- *Joint Ventures*: India has agreed to bind its recent liberalization measures regulating the ability of current joint-ventures to enter into new joint-ventures.
- *Real Estate*: India has agreed to bind its new regulations governing investments in the real estate sector.
- *Others*: The Indian government has formally recognised Temasek and GIC as distinct entities. They are allowed to each own up to 10 percent of a listed Indian company, similar to other Foreign Institutional Investors (FII), as stipulated under current Securities and Exchange Board of India (SEBI) regulations.

4.7.8 Trade in Services: The services chapter ensures that service suppliers in India and Singapore are guaranteed access into each other's markets. The key features are highlighted as follows:

- Market Access: Both countries may not restrict access into their services market by imposing quantitative restrictions (e.g. numerical quotas on services suppliers that are allowed in the market).
- National Treatment: Services suppliers will be granted the same treatment as local service suppliers, i.e., no discrimination.
- Domestic Regulation: The chapter ensures that domestic regulations governing the provision of services are reasonable, impartial and objective.
- Mutual Recognition Agreements (MRAs): The chapter

facilitates the freer movement of people. Professional bodies in the accounting and auditing, architecture, medical (doctors), dental and nursing services sectors in both countries will negotiate agreements, within a year of the signing of CECA, recognising each other's education and professional qualifications. This means that upon the completion of these mutual recognition agreements, Indian and Singaporean professionals from these five professions could be able to practice in Singapore and India respectively. Professional bodies for services sectors not listed above would also be encouraged to enter into negotiations for MRAs.

The services commitments made by each country can be found in the Annexes to the Services Chapter. There are additional disciplines pertaining to Telecommunication Services and Financial Services in their respective Annexes to the Services Chapter.

Generally, the benefits of the CECA will extend to the citizens, permanent residents, local companies as well as foreign MNCs that are constituted or otherwise organised in India or Singapore. Companies wishing to supply audio-visual, educational, financial and telecommunication services, through commercial presence in India or Singapore, would have to meet ownership or control criteria in order to benefit from the CECA.

Both countries have committed to liberalise various services sectors beyond its WTO commitments.

The sectors which Singapore gets preferential access include business services, construction and related engineering services, financial services, telecommunication services, tourism and travel related services and transport services.

India would be able to enjoy preferential treatment for sectors such as business services, distribution services, education services, environmental services and transportation services.

- For Financial Services, Singapore owned or controlled

financial institutions have been given greater privileges to access the Indian market. In banking, DBS, UOB and OCBC can each set up a wholly owned subsidiary (WOS) in India to enjoy treatment on par with Indian banks in branching, places of operations and prudential requirements. Alternatively, should they choose to set up as branches, they have been allocated a separate quota of 15 branches (for all 3 banks) over 4 years, over and above the quota for all foreign banks.

- For asset management, Singapore owned or controlled fund managers have the additional privilege of offering Indian investors mutual funds and collective investment schemes (CIS) listed on the Singapore Exchange (SGX) as well as exchange traded funds (ETF). These instruments offered by our asset managers are free from the restriction that they must only invest in entities which have a stake in Indian companies. India has similarly lifted this limitation for India owned or controlled fund managers. Both Singapore and India owned or controlled fund managers can also invest an additional US$ 250 million in equities and instruments listed on the SGX, including mutual funds, CIS and ETFs. This is in addition to the US$1 billion cap that all asset managers can invest abroad.
- Indian banks and financial institutions can take advantage of CECA to expand their activities in Singapore. To this end, Indian banks, that satisfy Singapore's admission criteria, will be given Wholesale Bank licences and up to 3 bank licences with Qualifying Full Banks privileges. In addition, India insurers and capital market intermediaries that satisfy our admission criteria will have open access to set up in Singapore.
- For Telecommunication services, India will bind its foreign equity limit from 25 percent to 49 percent for most services including basic, cellular and long-distance services and 74 percent for internet and infrastructure services. India will also ensure that telecommunication

providers from Singapore are treated fairly, transparently, and allowed to obtain access to the necessary public infrastructure in order to offer their services, thereby creating a more level playing field in India for our Singapore's telecom providers. On its part, Singapore has made binding commitments for telecommunication services such as Basic Telecommunication Services (facilities-based), Mobile Services, and Value-Added Network (VAN) Services.

4.7.9 Air Services: India and Singapore have reaffirmed their rights and obligations under previous agreements and recognise the importance of air connectivity to support the expansion of tourism, trade and investments.

Both countries will review and enhance further air services linkages through the bilateral Air Services Agreement, in future.

4.7.10 Movement of Natural Persons: The cross-border movement of natural persons plays a central role in initiating and supporting trade and investments in goods and services. This chapter enhances trade and investment flows by facilitating easier temporary entry for 4 categories of business persons from India and Singapore:

- Business Visitors who are holders of five year multiple journey visa will be permitted to enter and engage in business activities for a period of up to 2 months, which upon request, may be further extended by up to 1 month.
- Short-term service suppliers will be granted temporary entry to service their contracts for an initial period of up to 90 days in the first instance.
- Professionals employed in 127 specific occupations will be allowed entry and stay for up to 1 year or the duration of contract, whichever is less.
- Intra-corporate transferees (i.e. managers, executives and specialists within organisations) will be permitted to stay and work in India and Singapore for an initial period of up to 2 years or the period of the contract, whichever is less.

The period of stay may be extended for period of up to 3 years at a time for a total term not exceeding 8 years.

The Movement of Natural Persons chapter does not apply to measures regarding citizenship, residence or employment on a permanent basis. It also does not apply to immigration measures as long as these immigration measures do not nullify or impair the commitments made by either country.

The chapter will grant Singaporean and Indian Citizens and Permanent Residents guaranteed entry and stay in each other's country as business visitors, short-term service suppliers, professionals and intra-corporate transferees.

Singapore companies will have certainty when they choose to deploy Singapore staff to help manage their Indian operations. Skilled and qualified professionals and service suppliers from Singapore would also gain easier access to the vast Indian market. Similarly, this would also apply to Indian companies when they deploy Indian staff to manage their operations in Singapore.

With freer movement of business persons between countries, bilateral trade and investment flows should be significantly enhanced. Hence, companies from both countries can leverage on the chapter to drive greater economic integration between India and Singapore.

4.7.11 E-Commerce: Both India and Singapore reaffirm their commitment to promote a liberalised environment for electronic commerce. The chapter on electronic commerce addresses fair treatment of digital products, such as software, e-books and e-movies, coming from Singapore.

The Agreement also prohibits any imposition of customs duties on digital products delivered electronically. In addition, both sides commit to ensuring transparency by making publicly available all relevant laws and regulations affecting electronic commerce.

4.7.12 Intellectual Property: The Chapter on Intellectual Property (IP) Cooperation is focused on collaboration and cooperation between the Parties.

The Parties agreed to undertake and promote mutually beneficial cooperation in the fields of IP and Plant Variety Rights. These forms of cooperation could include the joint organisation of training programs, and collaboration on projects to promote the effective use and application of IP. The Parties have specifically identified their leading training centres: the IP Academy, Singapore, and the Intellectual Property Training Institute (Nagpur), as initial partners for cooperation.

The provisions on cooperation and collaboration in IP and training arrived at under the Chapter paves the way forward for collaboration between the Parties in the development of key IP programmes and IP infrastructure. Singapore and India benefit mutually in terms of potential exchange on IP and IP-related training and education programmes. In addition, the mutual recognition of the importance of plant variety rights means that both Singapore and India will be able to consider cooperation activities in this field.

4.7.13 Science and Technology: The Science and Technology cooperation chapter will allow for the fostering of closer collaboration in research and development and commercialisation of technologies between the scientific and research communities from the two countries. It expands an earlier agreement on science and technology signed in 1995.

The Agreement is geared towards harnessing the complementary capabilities available in the two countries. The areas of focus that have been identified for possible cooperation are marine and agricultural biotechnology, space research, advance materials and information technology.

4.7.14 Education: The education cooperation chapter is aimed at combining the strengths of the education system in India and Singapore to the mutual benefit of the two countries.

One of its key mandates is to facilitate joint post-graduate programs between the world-renowned Indian Institutes of Technology (IIT) and Institute of Science (IISc) with the Singapore universities. These programs will focus on research and education with clear industrial linkages to companies from both countries. Arising from this, NUS and IIT Bombay have recently signed an MOU to establish a joint graduate engineering programme. The NUS-IIT-B tie-up is the first alliance by any IIT with a foreign university in a significant manner. The programme will draw heavily on existing NUS and IIT-B infrastructure and course modules. Both IIT-B and NUS professors will participate in joint teaching and supervision of projects. The partnership is expected to yield some 40 MS and eight PhD graduates annually.

The chapter also provides that degrees specified by the University Grants Commission of India or an Institution of National Importance of India, and by universities in Singapore, shall be recognised for the purposes of admission into the universities of both countries. This is in addition to all other admission criteria that must still be satisfied.

A Joint Committee on Education will be established to emphasise the key role that education will play in fostering the relationship between the two countries. Its members will be drawn not only from government but from the private sector as well.

4.7.15 Media: The media cooperation chapter offers a platform for the regulatory agencies from both sides to work closely together. This will allow focus not only on regulatory issues of mutual concern, but more importantly on promoting greater industry and private sector collaboration. Some of the areas of collaboration that could be looked into are digital media and convergent services, intellectual property rights, education and training, co production of film and television content, distribution and marketing, and research and development.

4.7.16 Dispute Settlement: In any international agreement, whilst we do not expect nor hope for disputes between the Parties as to what the agreement means, it would nevertheless be prudent to prepare for such an eventuality. In this connection, Singapore and India have negotiated a comprehensive set of dispute settlement procedures. Disputes are subject to consultations, negotiations, conciliation and arbitration just like in the WTO, thereby enhancing the rule of law in international trade.

4.7.17 Review: The Ministers of India and Singapore, who are responsible for trade negotiations, will meet within a year of the date of entry into force of CECA for a review. Subsequent reviews will be done biennially or otherwise as appropriate.

4.8 Conclusions

The intermeshing of Indian and Singaporean areas of concern in trade augurs well for both countries. Singapore is looking out for viable and lucrative destinations besides China and the US, and India is well placed both economically and diplomatically to forge an effective and mutually beneficial partnership.

Thus the increasing diplomatic complementarities and synergies of the two countries in trade and investment, will act as a stabilizing force in the Asia-Pacific region.

5

India and Asia-Pacific Economic Co-operation (APEC) Forum

5.1 Background

The APEC (Asia-Pacific Economic Co-operation) forum is poised to become the dominant economic force in the dynamic Asia - Pacific region, where there is growing interdependence, based on growing trade and investment ties.

APEC has considerable diversity, and is far from being a homogenous group. The eighteen countries in the region have differences, which range from culture to legal and political structures, and to stages of economic development. This diversity of the countries in the region has been an important factor in curbing the creation of an institutional arrangement encompassing the entire region, where similar regional arrangements have progressed in other parts of the world.

The countries range from the small, but natural resource rich nations of Brunei and Papua New Guinea, to the large and economically powerful U.S and Japan.

There are the dynamic Newly Industrializing Countries (NICs) of South Korea, Taiwan, Singapore and Hong Kong, which have had the world's highest growth rates in this group. The rapidly growing second generation NICs of ASEAN (Association of South East Asian Nations)-Malaysia, Thailand and Indonesia are also members of APEC. China, despite its present low per-capita income, stands apart because of its size, expanding market and high growth potential. The South American members, Mexico and Chile have little in common with others, besides sharing a Pacific coastline and experiencing fairly rapid growth rates, although they have recently had difficulties in macro-economic management. Canada, Australia and New Zealand are the other three industrially advanced "white members" of the group. Within APEC, the distance between the richest and poorest countries is very large with Japan's per capita income sixty times larger than China, and the U.S and Papua New Guinea at almost opposite ends of the world's GNP table.

However, APEC members as a group have a dominant role in the world economy, as they account for 45 percent of world exports, 38 percent of the world population, 50 percent of world production, and 42 percent of global international reserves. 70 percent of the world trade is intra-APEC. APEC has also the world's major foreign investors (the U.S and Japan), and the major recipients (China and ASEAN).

5.2 Divisive Issues in APEC

Many trade and other disputes divide the member countries. The U.S and Japan narrowly skirted a full-scale trade war because of serious differences over protecting the U.S market from Japanese automobile exports. Japan recently slapped an anti-dumping clause on China. The U.S. continues to block China's entry into the WTO (World Trade Organisation) because the U.S. feels China's international trade regime is inconsistent with universally accepted laws, and has a poor intellectual property right protection mechanism. Japan, Korea and Taiwan do not want to open up their agricultural trade, because of strong domestic farm lobbies, much to the annoyance of U.S and Australia. Malaysia wants to push ahead with its EAEC (East Asian Economic Caucus), an economic grouping sans the U.S. There are also serious differences between China and Taiwan and South Korea and Japan.

The Japanese whose brand of "Mercantilism" is much criticised by the U.S feels that it can rally behind it the countries of North-East and South-East Asia, if there is a trade confrontation with the U.S., and is recently showing a renewed interest in developing an "Asian Consciousness", and projecting its version of consultative consensus in international trade dealings. However, there is also a conflicting trend of an underlying distrust for Japan because of its pre-World War II exploitative imperial record in Asia, and the fear of revival of the "Greater East Asian Co-Prosperity Sphere", with all its negative connotations. Chinese expansionism is also suspect. Its effective combination of defiance and deal making in its interactions with the U.S., despite serious differences, and its expanding military prowess evokes feelings of fear and mistrust among its smaller neighbours in Asia.

5.3 Open Regionalism

APEC was set up primarily as a consultative framework and an on-going process, not as a regional institutional grouping, or as a retaliatory exclusive trade bloc. The forum is based on "open regionalism" containing elements of both regional and global approaches to issues.

Regionalism is today fast catching on in the world. According to WTO, 110 regional deals were notified to GATT between 1948 and 1995. 1995 saw the accession to the European Union (EU), the world's biggest trading bloc of Austria, Finland and Sweden, and the creation of Mercosur, a customs union between Argentina, Brazil, Paraguay and Uruguay. SAPTA (South Asian Preferential Trade Area) has come into being in South Asia.

The seven ASEAN nations have agreed to set up a free trade area by 2003. Slovenia would join the Czech Republic, Hungary, Poland and Slovakia in the Central European Free-Trade Area. The EU and Turkey are due to set up a customs union.

Thus regional deals can accelerate liberalisation of things partially covered by WTO-for example the protection of foreign direct investment (FDI). Regional forums are also more flexible, as problems that would take years to sort out in global talks, can be dealt with in much shorter periods, where lesser number of countries are involved. Regional trade deals also "lock in" liberalisation, especially in LDCs (Less

Developed Countries).

APEC, despite fissiparous tendencies has come to stay as a viable grouping because of "Open Regionalism". This means promoting the integration of the Asia - Pacific region, while avoiding needless discrimination against the rest of the world. APEC by being an "open non-discriminatory economic association" has as its primary focus economic or more specially trade issues. It is also a "voluntary association" in which coordinated decision making is based on consensus, rather than an attempt to impose any supra-regional authority on its participants.

Traditional trade barriers such as tariffs or quotas need not be the only strategic obstacles to mutually beneficial integration of the Asia-Pacific region. The reduction of these barriers needs to be accompanied by work to reduce transaction costs imposed by uncertainties and infrastructure problems, as well as incompatible standards, regulations and administrative procedures. APEC governments should continue to follow the MFN (Most Favoured Nation) principle of Article 1 of GATT/WTO rather than trying to accommodate APEC through article 24 of GATT, which would lead to diversion of effort to convert APEC into a formal organisation delaying actual liberalisation.

5.4 Osaka Declaration

The "Osaka Declaration" or more specially the "Action Agenda" has as its defining feature "voluntarism" and "political determination" or as Malaysia prefers to call it controversially yet accurately "non-binding commitments". The "Osaka Initial Actions" and teeth to the Bogor declaration of resolving the developed APEC members to remove barriers to trade by 2010 and the developing members by 2020. The term "initial actions" reflects a political will among APEC members, who are required to officially reveal them only while declaring their action plans at their annual meeting in the Philippines next year. The fact that they have chosen to do so, albei in tentative form a full year earlier lends weight to the comment of the former Australian Prime Minister, Paul Keating, who said "it is the only body in the world that holds up prospects of general trade liberalisation".

The APEC has working groups on trade and investment, data review, trade promotion, industrial science and technology, HRD (human resource development), regional energy cooperation, marine resources conservation, telecommunications, transportation, tourism and fisheries. The APEC has agreed to permit non-members to participate in working groups as guests. Participation in the WG (working groups) must be clearly understood not to imply any tacit endorsement of future membership or observers' status in other APEC activities.

The subject that dominated APEC and the Action Agenda was that of trade and investment liberalisation in 15 areas, to the disappointment of the developing economies like Indonesia and the Philippines, who preferred greater thrust on economic and technical cooperation.

China agreed to slash substantially the tariff on over 4,000 items by 1996. The reduction of the simple average tariff will be no less than 30 percent. Japan announced that it will raise the number of tariff reductions from 400 to 700, including textiles, chemicals, and steel and non-ferrous metals, to be completed two years earlier than the January 1998 date agreed in the Uruguay Round of GATT.

Aspects of the APEC agenda include improving communications, reducing uncertainties, resolving disputes, harmonising commercial laws and regulations, setting standards, meeting global objectives and taking the lead in global negotiations.

5.5 India's Standing in APEC

India has to sit up and brace herself to face the emerging realities, with the centre of the world's economy moving rightward i.e. to the Pacific, and APEC poised to become the dominant economic force in the dynamic Asia-Pacific region.

India's isolation from the wider efforts at Asian regional cooperation is a matter of great disappointment. India's excessive preoccupation with sub-continental problems, the fact that she was a late starter in the liberalisation process, and the lack of diplomatic and commercial dynamism in cultivating ASEAN in its formative years, has resulted in a more reactive rather than a pro-active stance with regard to APEC.

India has recently sounded out countries like Singapore, South Korea and Australia of its interest in being part of APEC, after the current ban on its expansion expires in 1997. The Prime Minister of India in his Singapore lecture stated that "the Asia-Pacific should be the spring board for India's leap into the global market place.". In the market-driven export-oriented economy of the future, India has a lot to gain by aligning closely with the APEC countries.

However at the Osaka APEC summit it was decided that at the Manila summit to be held in 1996, non-member countries would be permitted to participate in working group discussions, but not at the summit-level conference. This does not improve any country's chance of gaining membership, but gives it an opportunity to network with other members and influence decisions. Japan, Hong Kong and Singapore are yet to device the criteria to be approved for new membership after the end of 1996, when the Seattle meeting specified embargo on expansion ends. It is still unclear whether new members should meet defined criteria or depend on various other considerations, first the new members will be identified and then the criteria tailored to fit their inclusion.

Nevertheless it needs to be noted that India has substantial trade with the APEC countries. APEC today sources 54 percent of Indian imports, and receives 45 percent of Indian exports. Trade with the Asian members of APEC is significant, with Japan and ASEAN accounting for a substantial chunk. The U.S is India's most important trading partner followed by

Australia, China and South Korea.

India also needs to be taken seriously since the country's wishes to achieve a share of more than 1 percent in total world trade. Even the World Bank has identified India as becoming the fourth largest economy in Purchasing Power Parity (PPP), terms by 2020. India's attitude towards East Asia will also decide India's admission into APEC more than the significant trade volumes.

More than 50 percent of India's trade passes through the Pacific. Thus it is interested in APEC and has a stake in the security and stability of East Asia and the Pacific.

The India parliament also should be taken into confidence about what obligations India's membership of APEC entails by way of tariff reductions. India should also take note of the fact that a surrender or loss of some of its sovereignty would be more than made up by taking away some of other's sovereignty. Besides her economic potential, military strength and physical size, in sheer geographical terms, India abuts on both ASEAN and APEC. China has a long border with India, and Indonesia is barely 100 miles away from the southernmost island of the Andaman's chain. Three of ASEAN's seven members have maritime boundaries with India. There are many native Indians in Malaysia and Singapore, and in cultural terms too India has close affinity with Indonesia and Malaysia. Non-resident Indian nationals are also playing a significant role in the U.S, Canadian and Australian economies.

5.6 India's Trade and Economic Cooperation with Individual APEC Countries

We now study India's trade and economic cooperation with certain key APEC countries: the U.S, China, Canada, Australia, Japan and South Korea with focus on ASEAN.

5.6.1 United States: United States is one of India's leading trade partner. About 12.2 percent of India's exports during 2008-09 were destined to the U.S valued at US$ 22.51 billion. Gems and jewellery and textiles were the major items exported to US. These two commodity groups alone accounted for more than 50 percent of India's total exports to U.S.A. Engineering goods, precious stones, aviation and aircraft constituted as top items in total imports from US. Leather goods and handmade carpets and handicrafts are some of the other major items exported to the U.S.A.

USA's share in India's total imports was 6.1 percent in 2008-09 valued at US$ 18.56 billion. The basket of items imported from USA is diverse. Fertilizers, non-electrical machinery, metal scrap and electrical machinery are some of the major items imported from USA.

USA is also a leading collaborator and source of foreign investments in India. Between 1951 and 1991, 3,143 collaborations between the two countries were approved by the Indian government with direct investment approved totalling Rs. 1,658 crore between 1975 and 1992. During the decade April 2000 to March 2010, total FDI equity inflows from the US totalled up to US$ 8.27 billion constituting an 8 per cent share.

5.6.2 Japan: Of the total Indian exports in 2008-09, 1.6 percent went to Japan, while imports from Japan constituted 2.6 percent during the same period. Project goods, electrical and other machinery, transport equipment, iron and steel, optical goods, organic chemicals are the major items of India's import from Japan. On the export side important items are gems and jewellery, iron ore, raw cotton, ready-made garments, manufactures of metals etc.

India's new economic policy on foreign investment has made India an attractive proposition for Japanese investors. From a mere 30 million US$ in 1991, Japanese investment rose to 1.18 billion US$ in 2009-2010. However unless India provides for reliable infrastructure with adequate, assured and good quality power, communication and transportation, and also skilled and disciplined labour force, Japanese investors would not turn to India in big numbers.

5.6.3 China: In recent years, Sino-Indian trade has gained rapid growth, the trade volume has doubled and border trade has developed considerably. However, compared to the size of their economies especially to their trade volumes, the proportion of bilateral trade is insignificant. The total trade volume of China reached 2207 billion US$ in 2009, in which Sino-Indian trade just accounted for 1.9 percent. It is expected that with a further strengthening of Sino-Indian relations there will emerge more trade channels and the volume of trade will grow significantly, particularly border trade. China has also shown interest in Indian technologies in agriculture, genetic engineering, computer software, and oceanology. India can also benefit from China's achievements in small-scale blast furnaces, small-scale hydroelectric stations and space technology. To make full use of the complemnetarity between the two countries in these areas will only quicken the pace of their economic development and mitigate their technological dependence on developed countries. Joint ventures with large investments like between the China Aviation Industry and Hindustan Aeronautics to develop civil aircraft prove that bilateral economic and technological cooperation has reached new dimensions.

5.6.4 Korea: There has been a noticeable change in the trade relations between India and Korea. Korea's exports to India, which totalled US$ 440 million in 1993, rose to US$ 8.67 billion in 2009. Korea's FDI in India meanwhile shot up sharply to US$ 631 million during the period April 2000 to March 2010. It is a case of mutual benefit between India and S. Korea. S. Korea stands to gain by finding cost-effective bases in India for its large business houses to produce low-to medium-technology items, which prove expensive to produce at home. India's principal exports to South Korea were mineral fuels, mineral oils and others; metallic ores, slag and ash; oil cakes; organic chemicals and aluminium articles. India's principal imports from South Korea include man-made filament yarn, plastics and articles, mineral fuels, mineral oils and products, iron and steel and copper articles. Not just the

Indian government Indian business too is enamoured of South Korea. As reservoirs of technology, the innovating S. Koreans hold promise for joint ventures of India's huge domestic demand. Korean companies have established manufacturing bases in the field of automobiles, household electric appliances, textiles and telecommunication equipment.

5.6.5 Australia: Bilateral trade between India and Australia has maintained a steady upward trend, though both countries realise that the potential for growth is much higher. The bilateral trade between the two countries for the year 2008 stood at US$ 12.79 billion, which is 43 % higher than in 2007. Indian exports to Australia were US$ 1.52 billion while Indian imports from Australia stood at US$ 11.26 billion in 2008. India ranked 9th as Australia's overall trading partner in 2008. India's share of Australia's total trade was 3.4 %. India ranked 4th in Australia's export market with a share of 6.1 % in terms of overall exports. India's exports have been diverse, but their volumes have not been large enough. Textiles and clothing have been the mainstay with pearls and gems, engineering goods, chemicals and related products, plantation, agricultural products and leather making up the bulk of the remaining trade. In terms of investments too, Australia has been taking a keener interest in the opening up of the Indian economy. It ranked 21st among foreign investors for the period April 2000 to March 2010, with an investment of US$ 418 million. There is growing realisation on both sides of the need to step-up trade, investments and dialogue. A phased agreement on the political agenda on the multilateral horizon and a renewed commitment to stepping up bilateral relations should provide a new orientation to the private sectors in both countries. From a phase of "benign neglect" the two countries have reached the stage of "realisation of the potential".

5.6.6 Canada: At Canadian dollar 4.62 billion in 2008, bilateral trade between the two countries has reached record levels. Canada's exports to India were valued at $2.42 billion in 2008, and Canadian merchandise imports from India were valued at $2.20 billion. Investment figures also indicated strengthening commercial relations. In 2008, two-way direct investment reached $1.8 billion. Canadian direct investment into India at $801 million was up 25 per cent from 2007. Indian direct investment into Canada totalled $1.02 billion in 2008, an increase of almost 150 per cent over 2007. The above figures clearly indicate not only the potential for growth, but the fact that, with the existing base, Indo-Canadian trade has nowhere to else to go but up!

India's major imports from Canada include wood pulp, machinery and equipment, asbestos, sulphur, potassium chloride, resins (polyethylene/polypropelene), news print and iron and steel products. India's exports to Canada include garments, leather goods, carpets, food, fruit and vegetables engineering goods, gems and jewellery, minerals, petroleum products, chemicals and allied products. Much of Canada's success over the past year can, in fact be attributed to India's economic and trade reforms. Canada's growing presence in India cannot be measured solely by its export performance as many Canadian private sector enterprises bagged lucrative contracts in cellular telephone licenses, and aluminium processing. The Canadian International Development Agency (CIDA) has now adopted a new country policy framework that will focus on Indo-Canadian partnerships.

5.7 Political Relations between India and the APEC Countries

India, seen through the cold-war prism of South East Asia was perceived as a country mired in sub-continental problems, steeped in poverty due to obsolete economic approaches and an unacceptable strategic relationship with the former Soviet Union. India has a historic opportunity to unshackle itself from these past misconceptions and demonstrate the necessary political will and capability to play a constructive role in the dynamic Asia-Pacific region.

ASEAN's support for India in the region though primarily

based on India's attractiveness as an emerging market, is also important in geo-political terms as a factor in China's containment, and an assertion of its autonomy vis-à-vis the U.S. in the ARF (ASEAN Regional Forum).

The U.S. and India have in fact congruent geopolitical interests in maintaining a fair and stable equilibrium in Asia. India also needs to further alter its perception that the U.S. has an interest in creating impediments in its overall progress. The U.S. has been asking India to share its strategic concerns in the Asia-Pacific, particularly regarding the challenge China poses as an emerging Asian super power, and also the possibility of instability and uncertainty in the Korean peninsular. The U.S. and India have been exploring the possibility of closer military co-operation since the 1991 Kickleighter proposals. The trouble with the U.S. is that it is not sensitive to India's strategic concerns in relation to Pakistan, particularly with regard to the Kashmir issue. The U.S. continues to view Pakistan as a frontline moderate Islamic state, and a strategic ally to counter insurgency and fundamentalism in West and Central Asia. It is not willing to accommodate India's concerns about Pakistan's nuclear and missile capabilities, and to accept India as a strategic ally, with the new equations in the post-cold war world. Pakistan has adroitly managed to keep India out of the U.S's. primary foreign policy concerns.

China's growing military and economic prowess also poses a threat to India, as also its nuclear and missile capability in conjunction with Pakistan. The U.S. again is not sensitive to India's concerns regarding China. However, at the same time India does not want to identify too closely with the U.S. confrontationist stance towards China, which may prove to be counter-productive in the relaxed bilateral context of Sino-Indian relations. The `Border Dispute' between the two countries has for all purposes between frozen, and there is growing economic interaction between the two countries. There is thus primarily a mismatch of perceptions and expectations between India on the one hand as an emerging regional power and the U.S. on the other hand as a global power, which may not be sufficiently attuned to India's sensitivities and concerns. Added to this is China's emergence as a power with a global outreach, hence, the differing perceptions in the Asia-Pacific region.

It is in India's long term interest that she consolidates her "Asian identity". The ASEAN resilient approach of consultative and constructive engagement towards China to deter it from pursuing an aggressive and expansionist course suits India's interest the most. India must also keep in mind that support for its ARF application came from the ASEAN economies, despite the U.S., Canada, Japan and Australia wanting India to soften her stand on global non-proliferation issues like CTBT before agreeing to India playing a larger role in the Asia-Pacific region. However, apart from the nuclear issue, India's diplomatic ties are being further strengthened with Australia, Canada and Japan who all recognise it as an emerging economic force in Asia, which can compete with China.

Recent initiatives taken by India have gone a long way in removing apprehensions about India's intentions and capability of her military in the Asia-Pacific region. Joint naval exercises with Australia, Malaysia, Singapore and Indonesia have definitely contributed to a better understanding of the realities. Strategic co-operation received further fillip when India and Malaysia signed a Memorandum of Understanding in defence cooperation. Malaysian Air force personnel are being trained in the use of MIG 29 aircraft. The India-Malaysia dialogue and the Indo-Thailand dialogue have agreed that co-operation should include joint production and development of defence equipment.

India has however to realise that despite removal of apprehensions regarding military capabilities, India is the only country in the APEC region which is not a signatory to the NPT (Nuclear Non-Proliferation Treaty) or any other nuclear restraint regime. India's isolation by not signing the CTBT is viewed with great concern. There may be pressures on India to endorse the South East Asia Nuclear Weapons' Free Zone (SEANWFZ) and possibly become a part of it. Even India's approach towards Pakistan will be expected to be compatible with overall confidence building, conflict-resolution, and preventive diplomacy culture of the Asia-Pacific region. India's relationship with Russia will be closely watched, as any new arms acquisitions and up-gradation. India has to articulate her security concerns with extreme caution. China and the U.S. can pursue their respective security and nuclear policies though they are incompatible with ASEAN's primary concerns, but India may not be treated with the same circumspection. India will evoke more respect in the region, if she acts confidently and pursues a more pro-active Asia-Pacific diplomatic policy, and goes ahead with her domestic liberalisation policies with full vigour, and strengthens economic links with APEC nations.

5.8 Conclusions

India should identify her "core competitiveness in various commodities of interest to the APEC countries. Niche markets should be developed in exports such as textiles, gems and jewellery and leather goods. New forms of cooperation like trade generating joint ventures and joint tendering for third country projects with some of APEC economies should be pursued with renewed vigour.

With the United States, India should intensity and diversifies her economic relationship. As India's largest trading partner and also the largest investor Indo-US interactions have very important implications for the Indian economy. U.S. involvement in the development of the crucial infrastructure areas of the Indian economy like power, telecommunications, energy and transport should be deepened. In commodity trade, besides traditional commodities where India has a brand equity advantage, new products like engineering and software exports should be exported in larger quantities.

With the near normalisation of relations with China, cross-border trade should get a boost and the vast Chinese market should be very attractive for Indian exporters. Cooperation should also be intensified in areas like small industries and the financial sector, where India has considerable expertise.

In response to the continued rapid progress on market reforms, Australia's department of foreign affairs and trade has sharpened the commercial focus of the country's approach to India, while actively promoting the full range of the relationship. The Japanese also are showing renewed interest in India, and investment which was a bit slow in coming to India in the past should accelerate in the near future. There are also immense possibilities for a fruitful economic relationship with South Korea. The competitive advantage of South Korea in ship building, port management and automobile manufacturing has many lessons for India. The "Chaebols" (large industrial conglomerates) also can share their expertise with Indian companies in their globalising efforts.

In order to strengthen her case for APEC membership, India should press ahead in economic reforms with renewed vigour. Greater liberalisation and incentives for foreign investment should send the right signals to investors in these countries. Full convertibility of the rupee, rationalisation of taxes, and fulfilling her international obligations, in the newly formed WTO (World Trade Organisation), should help in accelerating India's global integration with APEC.

India should also keep herself fully informed of the deliberations and recommendations of APEC committees. There should be regular consultations with APEC member countries in international fora like the U.N., IMF and WTO, where India should use all her diplomatic finesse' to align her viewpoint with these countries.

India has much to gain from APEC in terms of trade reciprocity. As Indian trade barriers are demolished in relation to APEC, it will result in APEC also removing trade barriers.

There are many commodities in which India and APEC may complement each other on the basis of their respective surpluses and deficits. One serious short-term bottleneck may be posed by the insufficient availability of exportable surplus from India in a member of items. This may be overcome by greater inflows of investments from APEC to India in line with the "flying geese" model of shifting comparative advantage.

At present, APEC does not take much cognizance of the existence of the South Asia region. Regional cooperation facilitates the process of national integration, as has been seen from ASEAN experience in its formative years. If South Asia can start moving ahead jointly, after burying mutual animosity and discord, there is no reason why it cannot turn into a more dynamic entity, which can evolve over time into a cooperative partner of APEC. Cooperation with APEC will also further reinforce the process of intra-SAARC integration.

On the part of APEC also it is necessary to recognise the huge potential of India, for investment-related trade with its large market and vast repository of natural and human resources, which can be profitably exploited for mutual benefit.

Thus, India's desire to join APEC will depend on her diplomatic skills, and the economic and political clout she can muster before the next APEC summit.

APEC should also move further towards realising a region-wide open economy, which will not only contribute to regional liberalization of trade and investment, but will also advance the goal of global free trade. At the same time, APEC should be willing to meet the challenge of maintaining a sound and balanced economic relationship between the eastern and western parts of the Pacific. Individual APEC member countries' active participation in further unilateral liberalization, open-regionalism, region-wide trade facilitation programmes and cooperative efforts for structural transformation would greatly expedite the process of meeting this challenge successfully.

When APEC leaders meet for their next summit, APEC should have taken steps in evolving into a positive force and role-model for global liberalisation through "open regionalism", rather than yet another threat to the global system.

References

APEC, 1994a; "APEC Economic Leaders' Declaration of Common Resolve", Bogor, Indonesia, November.

——1994b; "Achieving the APEC Vision: Free and Open Trade in the Asia - Pacific", Second Report of the Eminent Persons Group, August.

Balls, Edward, 1993; "Divining the Motives for U.S - Japan Bashing", Financial Times, London, 19th July.

Bhanoji Rao, V.V., 1994; "APEC Perspectives and India", The Economic Times, Bombay, 10th October.

——1995; "Issues Before the APEC", The Economic Times, Bombay, 20th November.

Canada, 1995; The Economic Times, Country Report, 9th February.

CMIE (Centre for Monitoring the Indian Economy), 1993, "55 Major Countries".

Dobson, Wendy, 1994, "APEC Cooperation Amidst Diversity", ASEAN Economic Bulletin, Vol. 10, No. 3.

Elek, Andrew, 1995; "APEC Beyond Bogor: An Open Economic Association in the Asian - Pacific Region"; Asian-Pacific Economic Literature, Vol.9, No.1.

Ganekar, Bhagyashree, 1996, "Indo - Korean Cooperation - A Blooming Symbiosis" The Economic Times, 26th February.

Garnaut, R, 1994, "Options for Asia - Pacific Trade Liberalisation: A Pacific Free Trade Area?" in China, Siow Yue (Ed) APEC: Challenges and Opportunities, ISEAS, Singapore.

Jayanth, V, 1996; "Unrealised Potential of Indo-Australian Trade", The Hindu, March 28th.

Jiali, Ma, 1996; Relations between China and India Towards 21st Century" ICAPS Conference, Hyderabad.

Khergamvala, F.J, 1995; "APEC Steps to Remove Trade Barriers" The Hindu, 18th November.

Malhotra, Inder, 1994; "India, APEC, ASEAN and ARF", The Times of India, 23rd November.

Naisbitt, John, 1995; Mega Trends Asia, Nicholas Brealey Publishing, London.

Reza, Sadrel, 1994; "Economic Policy Reforms in South Asia and SAARC - APEC Trade Cooperation", DEVINSA South Asian Reviews and Abstracts, Vol.7, No.6, Marga Institute, Colombo.

Soesatro, Hadi, 1993; "Implications of the Post-cold War Politico - Security Environment on the Pacific Economy" in Pacific Dynamism and the International Economic System, ed. by C. Fred Bergsten and Marcus Noland, Washington D.C.

Stockwin, Harvey, 1994; "APEC Without India - But All is Not Lost", The Times of India, 20th November.

Yoo, Jang - Hee, 1995; "A Future Perspective of APEC", Asian Economic Journal, Vol. 9, No.1.

6

Sino-Indian Economic Relations

India is a vibrant democracy, despite vast religious, caste and economic diversities. China's per capita income began to exceed India's in the 1990s, though forty years earlier, India's was above that of China. India had avoided the pitfalls of the Great Leap Forward and the Cultural Revolution, though after the Reforms of Deng Xiao Ping since 1978, China is way ahead of India in all the economic and social parameters. In 1991, the Indian government initiated economic reforms. India's market-oriented liberalization and removal of industrial licensing and controls resulted in acceleration of GDP to about 6 percent a year since 1991, among the fastest for any nation, but considerably lower than the Chinese pace of about 9 percent for the corresponding period.

6.1 China's Amazing Economic Success

China's amazing economic success is stunning the world, and China understands how to move with the times like no other country. Its aim is to be a middle-level developed country in the mid-twenty-first century. China is the world's most competitive nation, and its seventh largest exporter. China desires to modernize rapidly by attracting more foreign investment. However, it must be remembered that the share of FDI in total investment in China is less than 8 percent, reflecting the extent of capital formation in the economy. The entry of China into the WTO will make China a more transparent and less subsidized economy, meaning more market access opportunity in the domestic markets of China. India could be described until recently as a traditional "mixed economy" with a large public sector, but also lot of private entrepreneurship.

China by contrast has been for the most part a command economy, which until recently had a small private sector, and only recognized the legal possibility of home-grown capitalists a few years ago. The Chinese economy has grown at an average annual rate of 9.8 percent for two-and-half decades, while India's economy has grown at around 5-6 percent per year over the same period. Chinese growth has been relatively volatile around this trend, reflecting stop-go-cycles of state response to inflation through aggregate credit management. The higher growth in China essentially occurs because of the much higher rate of investment in China. The investment rate in China (investment as a share of GDP) has fluctuated between 35 to 44 percent over the past 25 years, compared to 20 percent to 26 percent in India. In fact, the aggregate incremental capital-output ratios (ICORs) have been around the same in both economies. Within this, there is the critical role of infrastructure investment, which has averaged at 19 percent of GDP in China compared to 2 percent in India over the 1990s.

The mantra of China is sharply focused on becoming an economic superpower and hence everything else follows-foreign policy begins and ends with economic policy.

China is creating a national economy, and the result is a massive and painful restructuring of industry and society. Competition across provincial boundaries is becoming a reality. As a result, the country is experiencing deflation, a continual decline in prices. As prices fall, the economy stagnates.

Chinese export growth has been much more rapid, involving aggressive increases on world market shares. This export growth has been based on relocative capital that has been attracted not only by cheap labour but also by excellent and heavily subsidized infrastructure resulting from the high rate of infrastructure investment. In addition, since the Chinese state has also been keen on provision of basic goods in terms of housing, food and cheap transport facilities, this has played an important role in reducing labour costs for employers. In India, the cheap labour has been because of low absolute wages rather than public provision and underwriting of labour costs, and infrastructure development has been minimal. So it is not surprising that it has not really been an attractive location for export-oriented investment, its rate of export growth has been much lower, and exports have not become an engine of growth.

In terms of inequality, in both economies the recent pattern of growth has been inequitable. In China, the spatial inequalities across regions have been the sharpest. In India, vertical inequalities and rural-urban divide have become much more marked. In China recently, as a response to this, there have been some top-down measures to reduce inequality, for example through changes in tax rates, greater public investment in western and interior regions and improved social security benefits. In India, it is political change that has forced greater attention to redressing inequalities, though the process is still very incipient.

In terms of the future prospects, surprisingly, both economies end up with very similar issues despite these major differences. There are clear questions of sustainability of the current pattern of economic expansion in China, based on high export-accumulation model that requires constantly increasing shares of world markets and very high investment rates. Similarly, the hope in some policy quarters in India that information technology-enabled services can become the engine of growth is one, which raises the problems of sustainability.

The most important problems in the two economies are also similar mainly the agrarian crisis and the need to generate more employment. In both economies, the social sectors have been neglected recently by public intervention. In both countries, the policy message appears to be the same, that the most basic issues are those that require to be addressed first, and if so, the other areas of expansion will probably look after themselves.

India has individual liberty, political pluralism, and the institutional framework to take advantage of globalization. However it is constrained by mass poverty, lackadaisical government, growing fiscal problems, and a poor physical infrastructure. China has much less degrading poverty than India, which has more trade and investment links, while Chinese have a superior physical infrastructure. It is rapidly conforming to global behaviour patterns, and creating an internationally accepted legal system. However it too has fiscal problems, hidden in the banking system, and political risk.

China's industrial strength and infrastructure, and its vast pool of skilled labour, make it a natural choice for the manufacturing sector. India, on the other hand, with booming information technology sector and its huge reserves of English-speaking graduates, is a better option for outsourced service and technology development facilities. China has been favoured heavily by multinational corporations (MNCs) for manufacturing, with only limited business process outsourcing (BPO) activity coming in from Japanese and Korean firms. As opposed to the concentrated outsourced services and R&D facilities found in India, China is the hub of manufacturing.

As the WTO and TRIPS agreements progress, the export orientation of each country may cross into the present domain of the other due to drops in garment quota requirements and strengthening of the IPR culture.

The key strategies of Chinese reforms was to first effect a massive increase in incomes in the rural areas, and then meet the demand for consumer goods by encouraging the growth of VTEs (Village and Town Enterprises). The VTEs met the demand for basic consumer goods in the rural areas itself. There was continuous decentralization, and a system of profit taking with punishment for default. In India, the agricultural sector still accounts for about 70 percent of employment, but its share in GDP is down to 25 percent in other words the relative per capita income of the agricultural worker must be going down.

China can assist India in her globalization efforts, by cheaper imports from China and using them to produce low cost products in India itself, through the joint-venture strategy. By trading with China, India can be a little more competitive in global markets. A strategy of engagement with China and facing up to competition can be India's policy for the future.

India must emulate China by taking advantage of its cheap, hardworking and skilled workers to leverage better in world markets. To compete effectively, India needs to expand its primary and secondary education, and give more emphasis to vocational education and training.

China is in fact "*many small markets*", rather than "*the world's biggest market*". China today has good infrastructure-railways, roads and airports-so there is for the first time substantial inter-city and inter-provincial commerce, as one city can compete against "backward manufacturers" in another. Consequently there is the rise of national domestic brands.

At the political level, the Communist Party of China, eaten underneath by corruption still survives. One day new attitudes will push aside the corruption of the old, and a new China will emerge. Beijing strikes hard against recalcitrant elements and dissidents-but dissidents can be muzzled-not their ideas.

Since 1978, when the great modernizer, Deng Xiao Ping began China's reforms, and later in the nineties with former President's Jiang Zemin's vision, China has moved rapidly in its growth rates. However the new Chinese leadership needs to move ahead faster in political reforms. To recall, Chairman Mao's words "*it takes only one spark to start a prairie fire*". The next spark should not cause any dramatic upheavals.

The share of manufacturing in China's GDP is 49 percent, and Services constitute 33 percent of GDP. The biggest current draw for international investors is the "*Western Development Project*" (headquarters in Chonqing), initiating grandiose plans for Xinjiang and Tibet.

At the geo-political level, Sino-Indian relations should rise above the present border disputes, and past tilts. Relations should be non-hyphenated, and stand-alone, not guided by any third country. India occupies a special place, as the land of the Buddha in China. There is also admiration in India for China's economic achievements. India has an edge over China in terms of intellectual capital for the future knowledge economy.

Some of the general strengths and weaknesses of India and China are enumerated below:

6.2 Strengths of China

- Confucian ethic of discipline and obedience.
- Authoritarian Militarist State, with severe penalties for non-compliance.
- Highly disciplined top leadership that implements decisions once agreed, without further argument.
- Productivity of Chinese labour is five times that of India.
- China has a system of incentives and disincentives at Central, State and Town-level for performance.
- Small-scale imitator of well-known brands, giving better quality for a lesser price, not the original branded manufacturer. Chinese "under design" products to make them affordable by poorer households. Those who can afford to pay more for superior quality do so. In India, established manufacturers are unlike the Chinese; they are conditioned by MNCs, whose practices evolved in markets that can afford high prices for superior products, and that suited an economy where capacities were restricted by license. China dominates export of labour-intensive products world-wide-India does not, except in gems and jewellery. Chinese manufactured goods exports, as percent of GDP was 18 percent as against 4 percent for India (1999-2000).
- China has a system of incentives and disincentives at central, state and town level- for performance and non-performance.

- Foreign investment in China is in land, buildings, plant and machinery. Of the comparatively small foreign investment in India, a high proportion is in portfolio investment, and in buying existing capacities.

6.3 Weaknesses of China

- Communist Party of China still dominating, with no democratic dissent tolerated.
- Chinese legal system has still many weaknesses for corporate grievance redressal.
- China has yet to adapt fully to rules and regulations of a free market economy.
- China has lax labour regulations, and workers in many industries have to toil for longer hours.
- Working conditions are tough, as workers stay in crammed dormitories inside industrial zones to work from 8 A.M to 8 P.M. They are not allowed to form their own associations at national or regional level. This advantage may not last long, as workers become conscious of their rights.
- China's entry into WTO will call for a "fresh look" at its global interaction and domestic re-structuring.
- Corporate governance too is not of a high quality, as transactions are not wholly transparent. Managers of State Enterprises indulge in various irregularities-like siphoning of funds offshore, which in many cases comes back disguised as FDI.
- Chinese capital markets too are underdeveloped-regulations are not in tune with free-market earnings. Foreign investors can invest in B-group shares-only at Shanghai and Shenzhen-and cannot indulge in A-group shares-meant strictly for locals.

6.4 Strengths of India

- A stable and vibrant democracy. *India's greatest achievement is sustaining a democracy in exceptionally difficult circumstances.*

- Wide use of the English Language.
- Availability of world-class scientific, technical, managerial and professional manpower.
- Established Western style corporate democracy and a functioning legal system for grievance redressal and contract enforcement.
- A growing and sizable middle-class estimated at 200 million.
- Our culture encourages risk without reward, and as our defence forces have shown, we can be extremely disciplined and productive.

6.5 Weaknesses of India

- Hypocrisy of our political leadership.
- Poor implementation capacity of our administration.
- Speculative mentality of our industry.
- Rampant corruption, stifling the delivery system of any constructive programme.
- *"Vested Interests" and "Entrenched Rural Hierarchies" hampering any societal changes.*
- Our bureaucrats and politicians have yet to develop awareness that more trade and intensified economic relations enhances India's security, power and influence.

6.6 India and China: Similarities and Dissimilarities

The similarities are striking. China and India are amongst the five biggest countries in the world in terms of area, geographical diversity, population, market-size and economy measured in terms of purchasing power parity. Both countries were colonized by western powers, and attained independence within a few years of each other in the mid twentieth century. They both pursued socialist models of development before opening up gradually, China from 1978, and India from 1991.China and India are presently the fastest growing major economies of the world, although the majority of the population continues to be dependent on agriculture. The state sector continues to dominate economic activity in both countries, with the role of private enterprise expanding fast. In both China and India rapid economic growth has widened regional economic disparities.

Both China and India face serious fiscal problems and ballooning domestic debt and contingent liabilities, needing major public sector adjustments in the foreseeable future. However, much of India's public sector deficit has been absorbed directly by the government, whereas China has relied more heavily on the banking system to fund the deficit. Therefore, while India has higher fiscal deficits, China's banking system has more non-performing assets.

Corruption is endemic in both China and India. However, in China it is more centralized around the entrenched communist party, which practically guarantees quick action. In India corruption is more dispersed, and outcomes less certain. Because corruption in India is subject to legislative, media and judicial oversight, it is less of a systemic risk than in China.

China has shown far grater urgency in privatizing and closing a large number of state enterprises, while India's privatization programme has floundered. While China has effectively lowered trade barriers, with customs tariff collections comprising only about 3 percent ad valorem, Indian tariffs are still amongst the world's highest. Economic decentralization has proceeded at a much faster pace in China, with local governments in China having effective economic strengths and decision-making powers; where as India's centralized economic control is loosening only gradually.

While China is a closed society run by a tightly knit communist party, India is an open, democratic society, with an independent judiciary and press. With political dissent not aired in the public domain, China has overt political stability, arguably difficult to sustain during a severe economic downswing.

Both China and India face major future developmental

threats: for India these centre on policies to enhance savings and growth rates to remove poverty within a targeted time frame; for China the threats are more institutional, with institutions, especially financial, legal and political, not in sync with the needs of a market economy.

China could overtake India as the next Information Technology (IT) power and business-outsourcing hub for countries like the US, despite its lack of experience. China's offshore services will mature within the next five years, and companies should begin looking at the country as a potential source for IT-enabled services. Lower costs (roughly 1/6th of US counterparts), political stability, strong GDP growth (8.9 percent in 2009), the country offers the kind of environment needed by interested global companies.

India-China bilateral trade crossed the US$ 51 billion mark in 2008 with China becoming India's leading trade partner. However, the top five exports to China comprise mainly primary or low value-addition products viz., ores, slay and ash, cotton, yarn, fabric, organic chemicals and precious stones. Her imports from China are electrical machinery, organic chemicals, iron and steel, iron and steel products and pharmaceutical products. India should move up the value chain, and export more IT-related products and pharmaceuticals, as it is doing recently.

However, despite China's better image abroad, *the image of Indians abroad is very high in complete contrast the image of India is poor-but improving.* The *Indian diaspora* has gained considerable salience abroad, a number of Indian US$ billionaires live in the US and are highly rated. Despite loud proclamations, foreign investors consider everything unfriendly about India-the government, the bureaucracy and the infrastructure. We have to change the mind-set and working of Indian institutions.

India's trade with China is set to grow to US$ 100 billion by 2010. Trade and economic co-operation hold the key to strengthening overall bilateral relationship. During 2000-01,

India-China trade volume was just US$ 2 billion, but rose sharply to US$ 11.3 billion in 2004-05. However, the trade basket needs diversification, from raw materials and products of natural resource-based industries. If the trade and economic linkages is to expand exponentially, it is imperative that diversification takes place in the commodity-mix. China and India between themselves produce practically everything, cheaply and with high quality. With high export growth rates-India and China is galloping, but they must also gallop in tandem with each other.

A recent study by Goldman Sachs shows that India will take a long time to catch up with China-may not catch up even by 2050. This is because China has a much larger base in GDP than India; therefore, even smaller relative increases in income for China would mean a higher absolute increase than India. This is shown from Table 6.1.

Table 6.1: What will it take for India to Catch up with China?

India	Year	Growth Rate (percent)
To catch up China by	2050	8.9
To catch up China by	2020	11.6
Average growth rate since	2000	6.2
Average growth rate in	1990s	5.6
Average growth rate in	1980s	5.6

Source: Will India Catch-up with China? Mohan Guruswamy et al, Centre for Policy Alternatives, New Delhi.

China is today the world's manufacturing hub. India should emerge as the world's technology and IT (Information Technology) hub, if it follows pro-active policies. India and China thus have a lot to learn from each other's experience, and can be dynamic partners, rather than competitors in the globalised world.

References

Chang, Gordon G *The Coming Collapse of China*, Random House,

New York, 2001.

Gary S. Baker, *Chug Along with China*, ET, 2003.

Jayati Ghosh, *Divergent Development Models*, Frontline, September 9, 2005.

Mohan Guruswamy et al, *Will India Catch-up with China?,* Centre for Policy Alternatives, New Delhi, 2005.

Saighal, Vinod, *Re-structuring South Asian Security*, Manas Publications, New Delhi, 2000.

Shroff, Minoo R, *China's Remarkable Economic Growth-Some Lessons,* Forum of Free Enterprise, Mumbai, 2000.

Tony Nash, China *or India? -It's China & India*, Economic Times, May 11, 2005.

Wadhva, Charan D, *Geo-Economic Positioning of India's Trade and Allied Relations: Perspectives on India's Experience with Regional Integration* in V. A Pai Panandiker and Ashis Nandy, Contemporary India, Tata McGraw Hill Publishing Company Ltd. New Delhi.

Yasheng Huang and Tarun Khanna, *Can India Overtake China?* Foreign Policy, July-August, 2003.

7

Regional Co-operation in South Asia: Prognosis and Prospects

7.1 Background

The idea of setting up an organization for regional cooperation exclusively for seven South Asian nations-India, Bangladesh, Pakistan, Sri Lanka, Nepal, Bhutan and Maldives took shape in the early eighties. After the preparatory work of foreign secretaries was completed, it was decided that decisions should be taken on the basis of unanimity of all seven participating countries. It was agreed that contentious bilateral issues would be kept out of the deliberations, and regional cooperation would compliment multilateral cooperation. Following the preparatory meetings at the official and ministerial level, a summit meeting of the Heads of States/Governments was held in Dhaka in December 1985. The "Dhaka Declaration" was signed by the participating seven countries formally establishing SAARC (South Asian Association of Regional Cooperation).

7.2 SAARC Charter

The main objectives laid down by the SAARC charter are:

1. To improve the quality of life and promote the welfare of the peoples of South Asia.
2. To accelerate economic growth, social and cultural development in the region.
3. To promote self-reliance among the countries of the South Asian region.
4. To generate mutual trust and understanding of each other's problems.
5. To promote cooperation and collaboration in economic, social, cultural, technical and scientific fields.

6. To strengthen cooperation with other LDCs.
7. To cooperate on matters of common interest in international foray.
8. To strengthen cooperation with regional and global organizations.

The second summit of SAARC was held in Bangalore in 1986. The "Bangalore Declaration" expressed concern at the deteriorating economic environment for South Asian countries, but there was no unanimity of view regarding expansion of the scope of SAARC for cooperation in the "core sector" activities such as trade, energy, money and finance. The Kathmandu summit of 1987 also had limited success in making specific commitment to enhancing intra-regional trade. Subsequent summits were held in Islamabad (1988), Male (1990), Colombo (1991) and Dhaka (1993).

The 7th SAARC summit at Dhaka (1993) was postponed twice at the instance of India. The postponement of the summit was due to the volatile situation arising out of the demolition of the Babri Masjid in India.

The 15-page declaration adopted at the end of the Summit in 1993 covered the following issues:

1. SAPTA: (South Asian Preferential Trade Area) for economic cooperation in South Asia by liberalizing intra-region trade. The declaration called for gradual liberalization of intra-region trade and stressed the need for necessary steps to be taken to begin the first round of negotiations to exchange trade preferences among member states under SAPTA. The phrasing of the declaration related to liberalization of trade among SAARC members, and the signing of the framework of SAPTA are considered by analysts as a major concession to Pakistan.
2. Terrorism: The declaration stressed the need for coordinated action to combat terrorism. The SAARC leaders said that high priority should be given to the enactment of enabling legislation at the national level to help enforce the SAARC regional convention on

suppression of terrorism. The member-states, which had not yet done, so were urged to do so before the eighth summit. All the member-states excepting Pakistan and Bangladesh have enacted the enabling legislation.

The declaration also endorsed the Integrated Programme of Action (IPA) on the eradication of poverty in South Asia, trade, manufacture and services, environment, population, shelter, children, youth, disabled persons, women's development, science and technology, drug trafficking, security of smaller states, people to people contact, and South Asian Development Fund (SADF).

7.3 New Delhi Summit

The Eighth Summit meeting of SAARC countries took place in New Delhi in 1995. The most important achievement of the summit was the agreement to operationalise SAPTA by December, 1995. However, the Indo-Pakistan hostility syndrome continued at the summit. The difficulties caused by asymmetry and related matters were on expected lines, but some other problems acquired new proportions. These mainly related to the two "general provisions" of the SAARC charter-one, decisions at all levels are to taken on the basis of unanimity and, two bilateral and contentious issues are to be excluded from the deliberations. These decisions were taken after due deliberations and were based on sound logic. India attached great importance to consensus principle, if only to ensure that there was no ganging up of the others against it. This was also a safeguard for others, for was it inconceivable that any of the five or six countries tried to seek to push to the corner the remaining one or two? Similarly, the bar on contentious issues was intended to ensure that SAARC did not get bogged down in interminable controversies and shift the focus away from the basic objectives of regional cooperation.

Of late, Pakistan had sought to generate pressure against the bar. This was part of its effort to internationalize its problems with India, especially the Kashmir issue-as against the bilateral approach favoured by India in terms of the commitment of the two sides under the Shimla agreement. It sought to win sympathy and support of the other members, saying that unresolved issues involving it and India had derailed the SAARC process and that the association needed to address itself to the solution of these matters, if it was to forge ahead on the path of cooperation. This time, Nepal backed it on the issue. India, on the other hand, was opposed to any change in the charter. Though the SAARC forum was not to be used for bilateral matters, the opportunities provided by the presence of the heads of the summits, could be used and had been used for informal but valuable discussions.

There is so much divergence in the political perception of the SAARC countries, accentuated by extra-territorial powers who are interested in extending their influence in South Asia, that the very fact that member countries of SAARC have recognized that they can work together towards mutual advantage is in itself a big achievement. SAARC is much rhetoric about economic cooperation, but very little in terms of concrete programmes of enhancing trade or regional interaction.

7.4 SAPTA (SAARC Preferential Trading Area)

In order to increase intra-regional trade, a framework agreement on SAPTA was finalised by the Committee on Economic Cooperation, based on a draft prepared by the Inter-Governmental Group (IGG) on trade liberalization. This agreement was signed by the foreign ministers of all SAARC member states on 11th April 1993 during the Seventh SAARC Summit in Dhaka. This agreement is an important landmark in the history of SAARC as it will go a long way in promoting intra-regional trade and in gradually removing trade barriers presently existing in the member countries.

The basic principles of SAPTA are as follows:

1. Overall reciprocity and mutuality of advantages.
2. Step-by-step negotiations and extensions of preferential

trade arrangement in stages.

3. Inclusion of all types of products-raw, semi-processed and processed.
4. Special and favourable treatment to Least Developed Countries (LLDCs). The special treatment to LLDCs include allowance of favourable percentage points, application of relaxed rules of origin, favourable terms of technical assistance, duty free access, deeper tariff preferences, removal of non-tariff and para-tariff barriers, negotiations of long-term contracts to support sustainable exports and provision of special facilities with regard to shipping and identification, preparation and establishment of industrial and agricultural projects, training facilities and support to export marketing etc., possibly linked to cooperative financing and buyback arrangements.

SAPTA is expected to benefit not only the LDC members, but also the economically stronger members because of pooling of resources and markets, lower transport and transit costs due to geographical contiguity, relative compatibility of capital and intermediate goods produced within the region to factor endowments of other member states, efficiency gains due to increased intra-regional competition, and amicable environment for political harmony created as economic ties grow stronger and consequent benefits gain significance.

Expanded intra-regional trade and joint ventures can offer larger potential benefits to South Asia, which comprises about one-fifth of the world population. Natural resources endowments along with availability of relatively less expensive manpower in the region at all skill levels ensure benefits in terms of larger markets and fuller utilization of production capabilities, transfer of technological and comparative advantages.

The opening up of transit facilities under SAPTA would also necessitate harmonization of trading and commercial documents as well as exact definition of the rules of origin of the trade goods. Both these developments would stimulate intra-regional trade still further.

7.5 An Assessment of SAARC

SAARC completed ten years of existence in 1995. The countries of South Asia have great diversity in the levels of industrialization. Thus, trade in industrial goods through advantages of increased competitiveness may not take place. However, these are similarities in the major exportable items where regional cooperation is beneficial. In Bangladesh and India, jute and tea are important export commodities; in Pakistan and India cotton; and between Sri Lanka and India, tea; and between all countries of the region textiles, garments and leather goods are important exportables. Trade in complementary items can lead to country/commodity specialization, sharing of sales and marketing information, and jointly exploring third-country markets.

The intensity of trade among South Asian countries is low and between ASEAN and SAARC sub-regions only marginally better, with a strong bias in all these countries to trade with industrialized extra-regional countries.

The intra-regional trade among SAARC countries is low because besides having a "colonial propensity" there is added disadvantage of the perceived "India hegemony" factor. The countries of South Asia fear that India, being the dominant economic power of the region, she would be the only beneficiary in trade liberalization and economic cooperation projects.

The political scenario in South Asia is complex, with both regional and extra-regional strategic interests adding to friction and hence limiting greater regional economic integration. The "Shared Security Perception", which is a sine quo non of successful integration in other areas of the world is totally non-existent in the SAARC sub-region. India has had major political differences with almost all her South Asian neighbours, with the exception of Bhutan and Maldives. Some of the problems are due to the colonial legacy of a "common nation", while others relate to ethnic issues, sharing of river waters, differences over extra-regional powers and their relative roles, and the very fact that India is geographically and economically the pre-eminent regional power. Thus SAARC meetings have been much talk and common intent of good will, but have not gone beyond peripheral issues like a common approach to drug trafficking, the environment, or a desire for a world free of nuclear weapons. SAARC nations have to work on the principle of the "lowest common denominator" and proceed cautiously through consultation, before they embark on substantial economic cooperation.

Analysts feel that cooperation among SAARC nations faces the following obstacles:

1. The present political situation in the region is not conducive to cooperation. The traditional rivalry between India and Pakistan and the political climate in other countries points towards the unstable condition in the region.
2. The security problem in the region remains unresolved. India insists that regional security should be tackled through bilateral talks within the region and without the involvement of external powers. India's views is shared by Bhutan and Maldives, but Pakistan, Bangladesh and Sri Lanka, view India as a security threat and favour the presence of external powers in the region.
3. The imbalance in the resource position among SAARC members is seen as an obstacle to meaningful cooperation. Mutual suspicion of dependency has caused the member states to follow divergent development strategies.
4. The inter-mingling of the people of the region remains elusive, and on the contrary, each country tries to maintain its separate identity.
5. Political instability within the SAARC countries is another reason for poor cooperation among its members.

Despite the drawbacks to cooperation, SAARC cannot be written off. The SAARC summits have started the process of regional discussion and cooperation which over a period of time can create lasting bonds of friendship and cooperation among member States. The future of SAARC, however, will be determined more by bilateral relations among its member States.

8

Pakistan, India and the SAARC

8.1 Pakistan and SAARC

As a consequence of the Islamabad SAARC Summit of 2004, and the Indo-Pakistan dialogue, Pakistan seems to be at long last looking for a realistic solution to the Kashmir dispute. There is thus a "Paradigm shift" in that country's "bleed India" policy. However, experience of the past shows that any forward movement in peace initiatives is followed by retracting to old positions of animosity and hostility. Pakistan often talks peace, while preparing for war. It is hoped that the "war of attrition" in Kashmir will be given a final burial. The raison-de-atre of the Pakistan State should change from being a "spoiler" of India's progress. Pakistan should not insist on Kashmir as the core issue and progress with talks with India sequentially, but veer around to the Indian viewpoint that talks should progress simultaneously on all issues, including economic co-operation. Economic co-operation can bind the two nations together, unlike politics, which will create further divisions and mutual distrust.

Whatever be the motives, Pakistan is moving at a pace no one had dreamt of before. The voices within Pakistan urging the establishment to look for a way out of the Kashmir imbroglio are feeble, but growing. This could mean that the high-pitched decades-old rhetoric is toned down. Negotiations, from a Pakistan point of view should be conducted with India on a LOC (Line of Control) plus solution that allows for some territorial adjustments and soft borders, and possibly a ten-mile deep de-militarized zone. While the division of Kashmir is unfortunate, it is better to accept this reality, than live with endless suffering that has consumed almost a million lives since the 1980s.

However, there is a growing feeling in Pakistan that the country is being made to give in too much, without anything in return from India. It is hoped that once the "composite dialogue" gets underway, the feeling that India is extracting concessions from Pakistan without commensurate benefits is put to rest.

In its assessment, the Indian government feels there is unlikely to be any change in Pakistan's position vis-à-vis India. Kashmir is not about to be toppled off its pedestal, and a significant component of the Pakistan military-intelligence establishment will continue to subscribe to the bleed India theory.

Given the poor state of the Pakistan economy, anyone who comes to power in Pakistan is likely to be more vulnerable to the same pressures from the U.S and other Western powers.

8.2 SAFTA and Economic Integration

The 12th Summit of SAARC took place in the context of complex social, economic and political developments globally and regionally. The slowing down of global trade negotiations under W.T.O, a "shining India", and in some measure South Asia, the success of formations like ASEAN, the increasing international pressure to combat terrorism and resolve regional conflicts and regional security concerns have contributed to making regionalism not an option, but a necessity especially among LDCs with a burgeoning growth potential. But in the past, SAARC nations have been lackadaisical about implementing the high-sounding commitments of Summit declarations. The question to be asked is –"Is there any reason to believe that the Islamabad summit has discovered the magic that will hasten the pace towards regional integration"?

As has often been pointed out, SAARC is after all a unique regional group in many ways and especially because one country, India constitutes a centrality that is physical, geographical and economic. And there lies the core of the problem. The strongest gains of regionalism naturally accrue to India. It is for India to ensure that smaller members of the region have a growing stake in regionalism as well. This responsibility India has taken seriously. For example SAFTA (South Asia Free Trade Agreement) envisages the liberalisation of commodity trade as a key issue, with trade in services following.

As critics have pointed out, this would have little appeal to smaller nations, which only feel threatened by the flooding of goods from India, with the removal of barriers. Little effort has been made to ensure necessary protection to the least developed countries of the region. It is here that enlarging co-operation in areas such as education and health services can create synergies. It is also a cause for concern that SAARC agreements on co-operation on other issues, which attract no barriers, have not taken off. In 1992, the "Poverty Commission Report of SAARC" set targets for the eradication of poverty in South Asia. All that has happened is that is that in 2002, another commission was constituted, that has come up with further recommendations. Nor have SAARC nations registered a commendable record in other areas of possible co-operation. Under the "Integrated Programme of Action", there has not been a single co-operative project to harness hydro potential in the region to mutual benefit despite talk of sub-regional co-operation through growth triangles or quadrangles between India's northeast, Bangladesh, Bhutan and Nepal.

Now we discuss the prospects of a South Asian Union and the stages of integration in the SAARC region.

The region actually has an edge because of its common history. Before 1947, we had a single currency and an integrated market.

As regards the road map to economic integration:

1. **Free Trade Area:** Agreement has been signed to set-up a SAFTA by 2006. This will involve abolition of quantitative restrictions and reduction of import tariffs to about 5 percent on each other's products.
2. **Customs Union:** In a free trade area, there are chances of

possible leaks in the system. That is a country could import a product, then re-export it to another country, where tariffs are higher -customs union will take care of all situations. In a customs union there is a common external tariff.

3. **Common Market:** All restrictions on cross-border movements of labour, technology transfer are removed. There is a sharing of capital, resources and management. Common patrolling of borders and investing agencies working in tandem. There will be open-borders with travel without visas.
4. **Economic Union:** In economic union there is a common currency, harmonisation of fiscal and monetary policy.
5. **Political Union:** Harmonise security and foreign policy Common South Asian parliament is also mooted.

8.3 Pros and Cons of South Asian Integration

Regarding the pros and cons of South Asian integration--on the positive side, Indo-Pak trade may touch US$ 10 billion within 5 years of SAFTA. Integrated economies and markets will make South Asia an attractive destination for FDI. It will promote the sub-continent's civilizational harmony and cultural contiguity. Free from the burden of regional dissonance, India will be better equipped to play a larger legitimate role in world affairs.

On the flip side, the disadvantages would be India would have to constantly bend backwards to accommodate other smaller neighbours. Also, India's natural strategic compass is broader than South Asia, and extends from the Straits of Hormuz to the Malaccan Straits, with a pre-eminent role as a global power. Open borders also may spell trouble-we will have a flood of illegal immigrants particularly from Bangladesh and Pakistan, which may retard the Indian economy.

Coming to the specifics of SAFTA, it is on the whole a welcome step, as tariff barriers in the region are all artificial.

However, the duration of the process is too long. The process starts in 2006 and continues for another 6 to 8 years before the tariffs are actually brought down to the minimum range. The pace is much slower than the WTO route, and not keeping in pace with worldwide liberalisation trends. Sri Lanka has a FTA (Free Trade Agreement) with India and Pakistan, and will be initialling one with Bangladesh shortly.

In the current global context of regionalism, SAFTA will attract wider global attention in view of the combined huge market size and the growth potential of the region in terms of available resources.

South Asia has multiple heterogeneities-namely geographical, economic, political and social. The region doesn't lack resources, but lacks initiatives for building complementarities.

SAARC region continues to remain a hub of poverty, large unemployment, and economic backwardness. On the macro-economic front, all the major economies suffer from large fiscal deficits; expenditure increases on account of defence and security.

SAARC was established in 1986 as recognition of the imperative for a wider and broad-based regional co-operation forum encompassing cultural, social, economic and technical fields. However, SAARC couldn't make much headway ever since its inception, as each country followed a development strategy independent of others, without any policy co-ordination. Intra-SAARC trade has made little headway so far. In 2003, intra-SAARC trade (exports+imports) was around 5 percent of the total trade of the region. India accounts for 71 percent of intra-SAARC exports (mainly to Bangladesh, Nepal and Sri Lanka). Bangladesh accounts for 36 percent of intra-SAARC imports, due to large imports from India.

Even if India is a dominant economy in SAARC it makes tremendous economic sense to enter into co-operation with India. Since India is an emerging fast moving economy, the smaller countries can stand to benefit immensely by accessing the large domestic market of India. It should give them great opportunities for developing their economies, particularly agriculture and industry.

However, we should also integrate investment with trade. Bangladesh will sell to India in a free trade environment Dacca saris or hilsa fish, in which it has a competitive advantage and ready demand in India. But; this will be a lop-sided trade practice, defeating the very process. If India invests in gas-based projects in Bangladesh, and later imports gas from that country, it will be much more meaningful in a South Asian context.

Apart from trade, there will be the larger "peace and stability dividend". There will be region-wide growth, peace and harmony and a more conducive environment for investment, employment, effective resource mobilisation and utilisation for all countries.

A breakthrough in Indo-Pak bilateral relations is more good news for the "economic health" of the region, and will vindicate intra-SAARC trade liberalisation. Pharmaceuticals, engineering goods, power and infrastructure are areas of immediate intra-regional co-operation.

Will SAFTA work in the long run? Today, NAFTA is working well, EU's (European Union) single market and single currency have been very successful and of course ASEAN is working very well. There is thus reason to hope that SAARC will also be successful.

As regards SAPTA (South Asian Preferential Tariff Area) introduced in 1995, so far a total of 5,550 tariff lines have been earmarked for concessional tariffs by all countries, and value addition norm has been reduced from 50 percent to 40 percent. SAFTA has been perceived as a transition from SAPTA, through gradual progress in tariff concessions.

The progress in SAPTA was stymied and marred by apprehension, especially in Bangladesh and Pakistan, regarding possible flooding of goods from India. The focus of the trade dialogue within the region is dominated more by the desire to balance bilateral trade, than by the desire to promote trade. This comes in the way of growth of trade and affects progress on SAPTA/SAFTA.

Intra-SAARC investments are not very significant. Instead of co-operating among themselves, they have been competing to attract FDI. There is lack of dynamism at present in the intra-SAARC trade relationship.

It is hoped with the thawing of Indo-Pak relations, and the operationalization of SAFTA, a big boost to trade and investment flows within SAARC will begin.

India and Pakistan have agreed not to levy import duties of more than 5 percent on products traded within SAFTA. The other five SAARC countries have also agreed to reduce their import duties by between 0 percent and 5 percent within the next 10 years. SAFTA will be totally effective only by 2016.

The intermeshing of Indian and Singaporean areas of concern in trade augurs well for both countries. Singapore is looking out for viable and lucrative destinations besides China and the US, and India is well placed both economically and diplomatically to forge an effective and mutually beneficial partnership.

Thus the increasing diplomatic complementarities and synergies of the two countries in trade and investment, will act as a stabilizing force in the Asia-Pacific region.

In conclusion, if hostilities can create nuclear powers in the region, co-operation will create economic powers.

9

India and the Indian Ocean Rim Association for Regional Co-operation (IOR-ARC)

9.1 Background

The IOR-ARC (Indian Ocean Rim Association for Regional Cooperation), the latest grouping, of which India is a member, came into existence in March 1997 after initial meetings, called the "Mauritius Initiative". It consists of fourteen countries- Australia, India, Indonesia, Kenya, Madagascar, Malaysia, Mauritius, Mozambique, Oman, Singapore, South Africa, Sri Lanka, Tanzania and Yemen. At the second meeting of the Council of Ministers of the IOR-ARC in Maputo, Mozambique in March 1999, it was decided to admit five more members: Bangladesh, Iran, Seychelles, Thailand and the United Arab Emirates. The Council of Ministers is the Apex Body of IOR-ARC; besides there are two other bodies: IORBF [Indian Ocean Rim Business Forum] and IORAG [Indian Ocean Rim Academic Group] (These come under what is called the non-governmental Track-2 initiatives).

The initial euphoria of forging Indian Ocean Rim cooperation is today on the wane.

It is claimed that IOR-ARC has enormous economic potential and offers considerable trade and investment opportunities. South Africa is rich in minerals and is a major economic power in Africa. East Africa has enormous tourist potential. South Asia has abundant skilled manpower and untapped markets. South East Asia is an Economic Powerhouse, and Australia is rich in natural resources and a developed country.

However, it must be remembered that the Indian Ocean

Region comprises a collection of economically diverse and disparate countries. It is characterized by significant variations in levels of wealth and economic development, economic and trade interests, including dependence on regional trade, and political interest in regional cooperation. Australia, Singapore and United Arab Emirates fall in the high-income category. Malaysia, Mauritius, Oman, Seychelles and South Africa are in the upper middle-income category. Indonesia, Iran, Sri Lanka and Thailand fall in the lower middle-income category. Finally, Bangladesh, India, Kenya, Madagascar, Mozambique, Tanzania and Yemen belong to the low-income category. These low-income countries, with the exception of India and Kenya are among the least developed countries of the world. A country like Mozambique with one of the lowest per-capita incomes in the world has little in common with a high growth country like Singapore.

IOR-ARC member countries actively participate in the global trading environment at the commercial and political level. Exports from IOR-ARC countries to all markets grew almost 500 percent in the 90s, almost six times their previous level, but Singapore-Malaysia trade dominates IOR-ARC trade. IOR-ARC controls only 10.7 percent of the world trade, and intra-regional trade amounts to 18.5 percent, and thus it is not in a position to dominate global trade liberalization. There is little potential for member countries of the Indian Ocean region to deepen economic linkages and increase trade and investment flows. Studies show that trade increases were not linked to the formation of the IOR-ARC.

Approaches to regional cooperation will therefore be heavily influenced by these considerations.

The history of regional cooperation suggests that regional arrangements involve a dynamic process, often developing from relatively modest proposals, when compared with their subsequent evolution. This has been the case with the European Union (EU), and more recently the North American Free Trade Area (NAFTA).

Regional arrangements vary in their scope and depth of integration. At one extreme, they may be no more than informal consultative forums. More advanced, yet still shallow, forms of integration involve preferential trading arrangements, which extend lower tariff preferences to members than to non-members. Preferential arrangements may also include agreements on investments, standards and other regulatory issues.

Deeper forms of integration involve the formation of a single economics area behind common external tariffs. Such arrangements may extend to national governments ceding trade policy to a supra-national body, and pursuing the harmonisation of their micro and macro policies. The European Union (EU) is such a type of regional organization.

Regional arrangements may be driven either by market or political imperatives, or more usually some combination of both. All regional arrangements and other forms of regional cooperation can be positioned along a continuum from market-driven, to politically driven integration. At the far market-driven end, would be integration in the South China Region (Guangdong, Fujian, Taiwan and Hongkong), where the economies of Taiwan and the Mainland, do not recognise each other politically. At the far end of the policy-driven arrangements, with little market basis to integration, are many of the formal economic arrangements in Latin America and Africa in the 1960s and 1970s.

Open Regionalism

The IOR-ARC is based on the concept of Open Regionalism, which is distinct from Preferential Regionalism .In Preferential Regionalism trade preferences are given to members at reduced tariffs. This results in a net positive impact on trade among members. It may also have a negative impact or no effect on trade with non-members due to trade diversion. Regional co-operation, which promotes the benefits of closer regional ties, but without any discriminatory trade measures, is open regionalism. Simply put, open regionalism is trade liberalisation among the member countries in the region on a most favoured nation (MFN) basis unilaterally without asking for reciprocity from non-members.

It is argued that open regionalism is a flexible arrangement that is more member friendly than neo-liberalist regional arrangements such as preferential trading arrangements, free trade areas etc. There are no laws and binding contracts and decisions are made by consensus. Compliance to any commitment is voluntary and there is no rigid institutional structure and bureaucratic set-up to specify obligations.

Integration of the IOR will depend on the complementarity in terms of resources, skills, markets, investment flows of the countries of the region, and policy reforms (particularly domestic economic reform policies), that provide trade and investment opportunities. There are no binding contracts, and decisions are made by consensus. There is considerable confusion about the implications and relevance of Open-regionalism. The logic of the case of economic benefits to be won by unilateral liberalization is weak. There is always reluctance to comprehensive reduction of trade barriers. With unstructured arrangements, coordination is limited. A dialogue-oriented forum will not be as successful in economic terms as an action-oriented regional bloc will. Project-driven confidence-building measures will not be sufficient to sustain a regional grouping.

The basic ingredients for effective market integration to support open-regionalism are not in place in the IOR-ARC. Only that part of the IOR-ARC that strongly benefited from FDI was South East Asia sub-region and to a lesser extent Australia. The analysis of trade flow statistics show that the expected spin-off of accelerated economic growth in these regions has not permeated the larger region.

9.3 IOR-ARC Agenda

In the current IOR-ARC agenda, there are projects under

various working groups. Some of them have made considerable progress and reached a stage of recommending various sector–related policy proposals. These projects can be categorised into two broad areas: (a) trade and investment facilitation and (b) economic and technical co-operation. The projects are on: standards and accreditation, investment facilitation and promotion trade promotion, improvement in maritime transport, human resource development, tourism promotion and development. The follow up on projects has been very tardy.

IOR covers too many individual countries, with significant differences in factor endowments. Similar economic structures mean limited trade opportunities. There are also limited complementarities in terms of savings-most of the economies are borrowers- and in terms of supply and demand for advanced capital goods and technology.

Almost 90 percent of intra-IOR-ARC trade and its growth come from the Southeast Asian countries. North and East African and Indian Ocean Island sub-groups have contributed only marginally to intra-IOR-ARC trade and its growth. The analysis of trade flow statistics shows that the expected spin-off of accelerated economic growth in these regions has not permeated the larger region.

The Indian Ocean group is much too disparate and scattered to make a mark in the near future. South Africa has its own African commitments, has a sagging interest in IOR-ARC and is overburdened by regional pulls in its immediate neighbourhood. There are renewed financial problems in South East Asia, and the economies have once again slowed down, after recovering from the financial crisis of 1997. Australia has a reluctant "look west" policy, and continues her close ties with the Pacific-particularly the United States. Moreover, Australia was interested in the IOR-ARC, more from a security/defence perspective rather than economic cooperation. Mauritius and Oman are active in the IOR-ARC, because they need more economic space to assert themselves. Mauritius is better known for routing questionable foreign investment through its shores to India-known as the "Mauritius Route". In any case such grandiose schemes of regional cooperation spanning three Continents-from Canberra to Cape Town, with Calcutta along the way are far too ambitious to be economically viable.

The influence of the Indian diaspora in promoting intra-IOR trade and directing it to India has also been minimal, unlike the Chinese and their strong GUANXI (networking contracts) with a lasting contribution to the development of Mainland China. Compliance to any commitment is voluntary and there is no rigid institutional structure to enforce obligations.

As regards the so-called Track2 initiatives, the IORAG also has not contributed much to furthering Rim cooperation. The Chair in Indian Ocean Studies at Mauritius is lying vacant for sometime now. External Affairs Ministry officials say that the academic inputs to policymaking were inadequate, but the fact is that South Block mandarins are also not too enthusiastic about the IOR-ARC.

Bilateral initiatives will yield greater flows of trade, than over-ambitious regional cooperation plans. To increase India's share of merchandise exports from the stagnant 0.7 percent to a higher level, sustained export promotion should be the constant endeavour of the government. These should include reduction in transaction costs through decentralisation, simplification of procedures, and identification of thrust sectors. Measures such as special economic zones, promotion of agricultural exports, market access initiatives, setting up business cum trade facilitation centres/trade portals and duty free replenishments, should be pursued with renewed vigour. India should further intensify her trade with the European Union and select ASEAN countries like Malaysia and Singapore, where there are new opportunities emerging in the post-WTO accord world. Bilateral Free Trade Pacts like India has with Nepal and Sri Lanka should be encouraged.

Thus India should focus her economic diplomacy on deepening bilateral engagement and FTAs (Free Trade Agreements) rather than in pursuing regional cooperation with an amorphous and heterogeneous group of countries, like in the Indian Ocean region.

10

India's Globalization Prognosis and Prospects

10.1 Introduction

Globalization gained momentum from the mid-1980s. The globalization of markets and marketization of economics, politics and culture was spearheaded by global capitalism. In terms of politics and international relations, globalization means a greater bonding or coming together of nation states. With the collapse of communism and the end of the cold war, the fading away of non-aligned and of the North-South conflict, nations are moving closer to each other.

Greater internationalization, globalization and integration seem to be the new order of the day. Regional integration is taking place all over the world. In Europe, the EEC or the European Economic Community has given place to the EU or European Union, where the twelve members have made further efforts at monetary and financial integration with the ultimate goal of full political union. The erstwhile Soviet Union in its new incarnation as the Russian Federation, and the newly liberated Eastern European countries has joined their former foes of NATO to form a "Partnership for Peace". In Asia greater steps towards regional integration have resulted in the formation of AFTA (ASEAN Free Trade Area), while new Pan-Pacific organisations like APEC (Asia Pacific Economic Community) and the EAEC (East Asia Economic Caucus) have emerged. In North America, the US, Mexico and Canada have joined to form NAFTA (North American Free Trade Area) while in Africa a newly democratized South Africa has joined its former front-line enemies in Southern Africa to revitalize the newly named SADC (Southern African Development Community).

Thus in international relations, globalisation has meant nations shedding their ideological and political differences and forming new alliances, and trading groups and increasingly cooperating in international arena like the UN and other world bodies viz., the IMF, the World Bank and GATT. Globalization in socio-cultural terms means opening up our society to influences, cultures and patterns of behaviour of other nations and trying to spread our culture and influence to others. In reality, LDCs and nascent modernizing societies like India are more prone to be influenced by external cultural influences than to export their own culture and value systems. This is because the media play a major role in the "globalization" or "internationalization" process. Now the print media from abroad certainly have a strong influence on our urban elites; but much more pervasive is the influence of the visual and electronic media: and in a traditional and largely conservative society like India, the visual impact of foreign life styles can be psychologically un-nerving.

10.2 India's Open-skies Policy

The open-skies policy of the government of India allowing foreign electronic media via satellites to penetrate Indian homes surely has a powerful influence on the social fabric of the nation which can be strained if rural India develops unfulfillable aspirations for the consumption patterns of foreign societies. On the other hand, the growing demand from rural India may also give a boost to the economy. Also, the adaptive response time may be reduced owing to better telecommunication facilities, so that in areas like medicine, science and technology and the latest trends in informatics, Indian society may well leapfrog into the future. In economic terms, "Globalization" means increasing integration with the world economy. It means, developing an outward market orientation rather than the inward looking policy of depending solely on domestic markets. Economic globalization means opening our doors and windows to goods, services and investment from other countries of the world, while trying to export our own goods and services to the outside world.

10.3 Autarkic Past of India

Independent India entertained autarkic notions of eliminating external influences and tried to cut itself from the global economy instead of seeking opportunities in it. As a result, India's share of world trade fell from 2.5 percent in 1947 to 0.5 percent today because of a conscious decision to de-emphasize foreign trade, the free flow of technology and foreign investment. India also got bogged down in the notion that aid and not trade was the stuff of which development was made. It failed to recognize that dynamic businessmen not clever bureaucrats would transform a backward economy. Until recently our response to the global economy has been reactive and negative. Our national economy has stayed on the fringes of the world. We participated in international trade only at the minimum, unavoidable levels, importing only what was absolutely needed and could not be produced domestically and exporting just enough to pay for these imports. Over the decades the Indian economy operated in a planned set up, within a framework of regulations and controls, with the public sector occupying the "commanding heights". On the other hand, the successful developing countries of Asia struck out another path.

They first developed their human though insistence on universal education and public health, fields in which India has done badly. Secondly, they recognized that entrepreneurial energies of their businessmen were a prime asset and encouraged them to launch forth, while we equated profit with sin. Thirdly they created an economic system where innovation and productivity yielded the most profit, not licence manipulation. Fourthly, they ensured that commercial principles ruled in the supply of basic services like power, transport and finance. We on the other hand have indulged in politically motivated giveaways, which destroy the very institutions concerned. Fifthly, they made sure that production for export was at least as profitable as production for domestic consumption, thus giving international trade a key role in development. Until the end of the 1970s, India's trade policy was basically guided by import substitution.

A trade regime with high protective walls and import quotas afforded open-ended protection to domestic import-competing industries with no comparable encouragement to exports. This created a high cost, low quality and high profit domestic economy. Entrepreneurs were stripped of the very desire to export, apart from being unable to do so, owing to the high cost and low quality of their products. Exports had, therefore, to be provided with many concessions like duty free imports, duty drawbacks, exemptions, from income tax and cash compensatory support. On the other hand, considerable progress was achieved in diversifying the economy through a continuous planning process with slow improvement in the GDP growth rate. Finally, in the eighties a tendency developed towards relaxation of the crippling regulatory system, in response to dynamic changes and growing pressures, both domestic and global. However, these moves towards deregulation, liberalization and opening up of the economy initiated in the and early'80s were piecemeal, not systematic, and not integrated into any overall policy framework. India's arms-length relationship with the global economy could not however continue indefinitely. In June 1991, the country awoke to the dire consequences of its closed, regulated economy. In was hit by a balance of payments crisis, being left with a foreign exchange reserves of just US$ 1 billion, enough for 15 days of essential imports. The country was on the verge of bankruptcy and default on its foreign debts. Simultaneously there was a decline in foreign aid. Hence, there was a desperate need to accelerate growth to seek foreign markets for our goods and services and to explore ways of attracting foreign capital and technology. In other words, India's own urgent needs required links with the rest of the world.

Simultaneously the world outside had radically changed.

Today, a large volume of economic and financial transactions takes place outside the network of government agencies. This has reduced the role of central banks like the Reserve Bank of India (RBI) and increased the role of MNCs (Multi National Companies). A sizeable volume of financial transfers across national frontiers today constitutes the internal accounts of MNCs in which they alone take key decisions. evolutionary changes in transport and communication systems, liberalized trading arrangements, the relaxation of foreign exchange controls in most industrialised countries and many NIC's (newly industrializing countries) and the diffusion of new technology had dramatically increased the degree of interdependence among nations, leading to an unprecedented increase in international trade in goods and services and in the volume of capital and technology flows, benefiting the participating countries enormously the same time, this interdependence has reduced the area over which domestic policy used to exercise sole control. In other words, the individual countries have become more amenable or rather more vulnerable to external influences. Even the most powerful economies find that there are limits to governmental action. India is obviously even more vulnerable. Clearly, national interest demanded that we accept the world as it is and looked for opportunities to strengthen our economy and gradually outgrow the league of minor players. Any other course would have been suicidal. Now, greater participation in the global economy means that we have to learn the rules of the game of globalisation and how to use them to our advantage.

10.4 Preamble to New Economic Policy

Trade policies had been somewhat liberalised during the 1980s and three long term export-import (EXIM) policies had been announced by the government – the first in 1985, the second in 1988 and the third in 1990. Import licensing was considerably liberalized to provide domestic producers access to cheaper capital goods, intermediates and raw materials and to help them upgrade technology. A number of items were placed in the OGL (Open General Licence) list and required no import licence since July 1991, however, policies have moved consistently towards deregulation, liberalization and globalization of the economy on an irreversible basis. The major changes in policy fall under five heads-Industrial, Trade, Financial, Fiscal and Monetary. We will concentrate on the trade policy reforms, since these are crucial in the globalization efforts of India.

The new government first undertook a comprehensive review of the existing export and import policy, and announced major structural trade reforms on July 4, 1991 and subsequently on August 13, the same year. These reforms aimed at vigorous elimination or reduction of import licensing, encouragement to exports and promotion of savings. The main features of this policy were as follows: A new EXIM Scrip System enabling easier imports; grant of additional licenses to manufacture; decanalisation of imports and exports, enabling private parties to enter and abolition of Cash Compensatory Support (CCS) for exports.

On March 31, 1992 the Commerce Ministry announced a stable liberalized export-import policy for the next five years (1992-1997). Trade would be free, subject to only a small negative list of exports. The basic aim was to strengthen liberalisation policies and to make trade policies simple, transparent and easy to administer. The negative list of imports is the smallest ever; three items were banned, 68 items restricted and only eight items canalised through public sector trading houses. The negative list of exports was pruned with only seven items banned 62 items subject to restrictions and 10 items canalised. Import of capital goods was liberalized and no longer remained on the negative list. EPCG (Export Promotion of Capital Goods) scheme was liberalized and extended to components of capital goods with a concessional customs duty of 15 percent.

Imports of raw materials were also liberalised and barring a few items, raw materials no longer appear in the negative list. The definition of 'deemed exports' was clarified. The following three kinds of organisations are now eligible for special import licences—(a) Export Houses, (b) Trading Houses, (c) Manufacturers with ISO 9000 or BIS 14000 certification. A national campaign for quality awareness was to be launched and laboratories and testing houses were to be upgraded and accredited. Concurrent policy reforms were made with regard to Industrial Policy; the Public Sector; Factor Markets, including labour, capital and the financial sector; Tariff policy and the 'Administered Price' policy. The structural reforms in the spheres of trade, industry, finance and the public sector were expected to impart dynamism and efficiency to the growth process and to provide a solid foundation for industrial revival and for acceleration of India's globalisation efforts.

10.5 Aspects of Economic Globalization

10.5.1 Foreign Trade and Investment: Our global trade pattern since 1991 is more or less in consonance with political and economic developments the world over. Exports to GCA (general currency areas) have increased. With the collapse of the Soviet Union and the growing turmoil in the newly liberated economies of Eastern Europe, both our exports and imports to and from this region have drastically declined. As a result foreign trade in Rupee terms has virtually disappeared. One favourable aspect of this development is that we now earn more hard currency. Besides we have been obliged to improve the quality of our products greatly.

While we should strengthen our position in the US and Western Europe, it is now high time for Indian business to fan out to new regions of the world. In South East Asia, Malaysia is becoming saturated with Indian ventures and hence we should make further inroads into Thailand, Singapore and the

Indo-Chinese countries. In Africa, the Francophone West African countries have been almost ignored; though there does exist scope for an Indian commercial presence. South America and the Caribbean countries can also be explored for Indian expertise and managerial contributions particularly in regard to small-scale industries. Similarly there are good prospects once Russia opens up Siberia for international ventures. Eastern Europe offers immense possibilities for our private sector companies to establish production-sharing arrangements. The government of India has identified 34 export thrust areas where Indian products should do well, such as marine products, horticulture, floriculture, jewellery, bicycles and granite. Export units in these areas are being provided infrastructural support and development assistance to increase their existing strengths.

It is important to concentrate on a few products where we have a competitive advantage rather than try to make market inroads with an amorphous group of products. It has to be kept in mind that in the new EU (European Union) there will be an increasing demand for "branded goods" with appeal to specific categories of consumers. At the same time, customers around the world will look for products with special fashion appeal. Thus "niche marketing" will become increasingly important. In our view India has the potential to carve out exclusive "niches" for itself in leather garments for up-market consumers in Europe and in designer cotton wear for the younger generation in the US and Western Europe. Food processing and computer software are also areas which hold a lot of promise for India's overseas business forays.

10.5.2 Right Selection of Personnel: Besides, the product profile and country spectrum, an important aspect in globalisation efforts is manpower training. The selection of personnel to go abroad should be very carefully done. Only the best managers who have worked competently in various functional areas at home should be sent abroad. The mindset of people sent abroad should be such that they are equally competent to work in an alien milieu. Thus a common complaint among Japanese and South Korean business undertakings is that Indian businessmen are overbearing in their dealings and have a supercilious attitude. It has to be realised that while keeping pace with the West may be important, the grace of the East has to be given due consideration if we want to succeed in East Asia. This requires proper orientation and cross-cultural training prior to an overseas assignment. The manager working abroad has to deal with people with different value systems, inter-personal behaviour patterns and work practices. He has to interact with such business associates in a culturally appropriate manner. This calls for adequate orientation and training in languages, legal procedures, and customs and above all in suitable reactions and responses so that the sensitivities of the host are always respected.

10.5.3 Monitoring and Feedback: A major weakness in our globalisation strategies is improper monitoring and inadequate feedback. Our diplomatic missions through the commercial attaches should take greater interest in our foreign business presence. They should constantly give feedback to the government of India on the progress of business ventures so that appropriate policy redirections can be attempted. "Country Risk Analysis" should be an integral part of the international business divisions of companies global checklist of the performance of enterprises in various regions of the world should be made, so that lessons can be learnt from both successes and failures coordinated country-specific policy evaluation of both private and public sector overseas ventures should be made, so that lessons can be learnt from both successes and failures.

A coordinated country-specific policy evaluation of both private and public sector overseas ventures should be undertaken by the Commerce Ministry in style of the celebrated Japanese MITI (Ministry of International Trade and Industry). This synergetic networking of expertise can be immensely useful in strengthening our globalisation efforts. India also has several overseas joint ventures, which promote not only trade but also investment-based economic cooperation. These joint ventures are in diverse fields and in many countries particularly in West Asia and South East Asia. Along with these joint ventures, collaborations in the form of consultancies transfer of know-how and management skills have acquired new dimensions. Indian ventures have made efforts to adapt first world technology to the needs of the third world and to impart management know-how in diverse fields including power generation, construction of civil projects, railway operation and other technical services. Such consultancies have been successful in Africa and West Asia. They need to be expanded.

10.6 Looking Ahead

Globalization involves both interdependence and integration with the rest of the world. Globalization is an attempt by India to join the industrialized and free market economies of the world. It involves discarding the traditional approaches to managing the economy and a massive social and economic experiment with little parallels in history. The "Strategic Intent" of India must be to become one of the Sixth largest economies of the world. Accomplishment of "strategic intent" of joining a select group of leading economies, calls for effective leadership, political will and a shared national agenda. It must be remembered that India has several advantages:

1. A stable and vibrant democracy.
2. Wide use of the English Language.
3. Availability of world class scientific, technical, managerial and professional manpower.
4. Established Western style corporate democracy and a functioning legal system for grievance redress and contract enforcement.
5. A growing and sizable middle-class estimated at 200

million.

India should effectively capitalize on these advantages in its quest to globalize. India's experiment with hybrid markets – not centrally planned or subject to market mechanisms may create structural impediments to change. India can rapidly build on its private sector capabilities, and public sector physical infrastructure. However, transition to a market economy will demand that processes that distorted market forces during the last thirty-five years –"the licence-quota Raj" be eliminated. The recent developments against globalization in Geneva, Seattle, Washington, Prague or Davos have proved that there is an alliance between ultra leftist as well as ultra rightist militants with narrow nationalist outlooks. Indian farmers were joined by Swiss farmers having opposite interests at the WTO meetings in Geneva in 1999. It should however be kept in mind that the former should benefit from liberalisation of agricultural trade unlike the latter who, with the Japanese are the most protected farmers in the world.

It should also be noted that foreign investors and MNCs are not waiting to rush into India, but they have to be assiduously courted, as there is worldwide competition for foreign capital. MNCs no longer represent the demonic face of capitalism today. Massive public funds are needed for much better operations and maintenance expenditure in the power and transport sectors. The miserable conditions of power supply in Kerala or New Delhi or deteriorating network of roads all over India require massive public investments which cannot be got by domestic investment alone. Globalization is not solely responsible for the poverty still prevailing in the LDCs. In India, one hears complaints of the lack of a 'human face' to economic reforms.

In "Green Revolution" villages, poverty is retreating and reforms favour the overall movement of the economy. In sluggish areas, reforms are hardly felt and conditions of the poor hardly change. The 'Roots' of poverty have little to do with globalization and reforms. Questions have to be asked to local politicians about the failure of 'reforms' in their States. The plains of Bihar could again be the granaries of India as they were with Bengal for a few thousand years till the end of the nineteenth century if proper policies are enforced. In the past ten years, India has been removing barriers to trade, FDI and foreign financial investment. The open market-guided economy has been far more efficient than the command economy. The economy has being growing at a steady growth rate of over 8 percent, experiencing only moderate inflation and taking all kinds of shocks–the East Asian and Russian crashes, rising oil prices and the recent global financial crisis, in its stride. There has been a perceptible increase in FDI, foreign collaborations and NRI investments.

It should be kept in mind that while the "Nehruvian Strategy" had historical significance giving the Indian economy a certain depth and spread, and lent the Indian economy and society the dignity it did not possess after the colonial experience it had negative features, which required a change in strategy. Over time connections were rewarded rather than entrepreneurial flair. Crony capitalism rather than socialism distorted the production structure. Today there is abroad consensus across the political spectrum that reforms should continue, although there are differences in the pace and sectoral calibration. Globalization has to be to our advantage and we should be clever enough to exploit the needs of the industrialized world and play one mega unit against the other. When an integrated pattern of relationship between different sectors in industry and trade emerges our economy will itself become Global in the true sense.

Foreign investment no longer represents the demonic face of capitalism. While concepts of sovereignty are changing in an increasingly interdependent globalised world, foreign companies are more than careful in conforming to legal codes and national laws in their host countries. The Chinese who not long ago, accused foreigners of being the running dogs of imperialism, who should be wiped out from the face of the earth, are now welcoming foreign investment with open arms. Today there is a realisation that in a competitive environment, effort, enterprise and innovation can bring about economic transformation. Criticisms about the new directions in economic policy have come both from left-leaning academicians and ultra-right wing parties. It is indeed ironic that while the Marxists in Government have realized the importance of the market mechanism to allocate resources, some left-wing academicians and leading intellectuals in our left-of-centre universities have raised unwarranted criticisms against economic reforms. These "drawing room Cassandra's" and "arm-chair Marxists", who are now bereft of any ideological moorings, with the demise of Communism, and who are denied lucrative foreign assignments or Government sinecures, like in the planning commission, have taken up Government-baiting as their principal occupation.

It must also be remembered that everything is not hunky-dory with economic reforms or the direction in which our polity is heading under the current dispensation. While at the macro-economic policy level the reforms are progressing in a reasonably satisfactory manner, it is at the micro – implementation level of translating policy into reality, that there are serious lacunae, which can derail the entire globalization-reform process. Senior-level bureaucrats are not ready to give up their discretionary powers to arbitrate between producers and consumers, while lower-level functionaries continue to play an obstructionist role. Inter-ministerial co-ordination needs to be fine-tuned much more. Our grass-root institutions need drastic over-hauling to see that the benefits of reforms and globalization percolate down to the poorer sections, and should be more accountable and responsive to their needs. Politicians in power (besides a few committed ministers and chief ministers) continue to behave in a feudal manner. Corruption, nepotism and vast "patronage networks" still exist. The colonial mind-set still pervades many of our Leaders and bureaucrats, who believe in a patron-client relationship of granting favours to stay in power and wielding influence, rather than service to the people as their representatives. There is need for serious introspection by our policy-makers, if India wants to be in the front ranks in the comity of nations.

10.7 Conclusions

India can strive to become a global player if it keeps in mind the following factors:

1. Develop a pro-active mind-set and agenda for effective globalization.
2. Target specific industries for special concessions.
3. Focus on quality as a national priority.
4. Allow Indian firms to invest in building marketing and service infrastructure in select markets.
5. Recognise bad loans and clean up the banking system.
6. Pay attention to the political processes in the industrialised countries.
7. Build up a strong anti-dumping secretariat outside the government to collect data on international costs and profitability in the production of consumer goods that will soon be freed from QRs (Quantitative Restrictions).
8. Reform of the Labour market and a proper exit policy for loss-making enterprises.

In the final analysis, a strong and vibrant democracy with women, rural poor and the oppressed classes waking up to the realization of the assertion of political power, can take a Globalize India to greater economic heights.

11

World Trade Organization (WTO) and the Uruguay Round

11.1 Introduction

The WTO is the only international body dealing with the rules of trade between nations. At its heart are the WTO agreements, negotiated and signed by the bulk of the World's trading nations. The WTO was established in 1995, as part of the Uruguay Round of Trade Negotiations. The three main purposes of WTO are:

- To help trade flow as freely as possible,
- To provide a forum for trade negotiations, and
- Settling trade disputes—the dispute settlement mechanism.

The Uruguay Round of MTNs (Multilateral Trade Negotiations) was launched at Punta del Este in Uruguay in 1986 at the ministerial level GATT meeting.

The main objective of GATT meetings is to expand international trade, and remove obstacles to the free flow of trade between nations. The Uruguay Round is the eighth in the GATT series of negotiations. Some other well-known rounds were the Kennedy Round and the Tokyo Round.

The Uruguay Round covers a much wider ambit of issues than MTNs. There are two simultaneous tracks, than earlier MTNs. There are two simultaneous tracks of negotiations GNG (Group of Negotiations on Goods) and GNS (Group of Negotiations on Services). In fact this is the first time that services have been brought in, mainly on the insistence of the United States which has the most to gain from their inclusion.

The GNG covers fourteen areas related to trade in goods. These include (1) Tariffs, (2) Non-Tariff Barriers (NTBs), (3) Products, (4) Natural resource-based products, (5) Textiles and Clothing, (6) Agriculture, (7) GATT articles, (8) Safeguards,

(9) MTN agreements and arrangements, (10) Subsidies and countervailing measures, (11) Dispute Settlement, (12) Trade-related Intellectual Property Rights (TRIPS). The TRIPS negotiations include trade in counterfeit goods and would develop a multilateral framework of principles, rules and disciplines dealing with international trade in counterfeit goods.

The negotiations must also develop effective and adequate protection of intellectual property rights, (13) Investment Measures (TRIMS). These negotiations were to examine existing GATT articles on trade restricting and distorting effects of investment measures and develop further provisions to prevent such adverse effects, and (14) Functioning of the GATT System (FOGS).

A GNS was simultaneously established to oversee negotiations on liberalising trade in services. The objective was to expand trade in services under conditions of transparency and liberalisation.

The Uruguay Round was scheduled to be completed by 1990that is within four years after commencement. However, even after seven years, that is 1993, the negotiations have still not concluded. It was this stalemate that prompted an intervention by the Director General of GATT, Mr. Arthur Dunkel to break the deadlock on contentious issues. This is called the Dunkel Draft or Dunkel Package, also derisively called DDT (Dunkel Draft Treaty).

11.2 Dunkel Proposals

We will now discuss some of the Dunkel proposals. We will first discuss the reintegration of textiles into the GATT framework. Trade in textiles and clothing has till now been governed by the multi fibre agreement (MFA) in force since 1974. Third-world countries which are large exporters of textiles face quotas imposed under MFA. The Dunkel Draft proposes a phasing out of these quotas over a period of ten years. After a fresh agreement enters into force (say in 1994),

16 percent of the textile sector will be integrated into GATT, with larger shares being integrated each year. However, the definition of textiles itself is widened to cover a larger range of products.

Negotiations on trade-disorienting agricultural policies were stalled for several months due to difference between the European Community (EC) and the US over farm subsidies. Studies have shown that there will be substantial gains once agricultural trade is liberalised. The contentious issue is the heavy subsidy given by the EC countries for production and export of basic agricultural foodstuffs. The Dunkel proposals call for reduction in domestic and export subsidies; and replacement of non-tariff barriers, like quotas and quantitative restrictions by tariffs. The deadlock between the US and EC appeared to have been resolved last summer with the two reaching agreement (The Blair House Accord) on contentious issues. Now, however, France has reneged under pressure from its farmers and the whole accord is in jeopardy. Some third world countries have argued that government measures to encourage agricultural and rural development form an integral part of development programmes, and should, therefore, not come under the purview of GATT. The Dunkel Draft does have preferential treatment for LDCs with regard to agriculture. All investment subsidies have been given an across the board exemption and input subsidies to low income producers have also been exempted.

In the negotiations on TRIMS, there have been differences among the developed countries, and the third world with regard to the export obligations imposed on industries. LDCs have argued that export commitments do not inhibit trade. Most of the policies with regard to TRIMS would be acceptable to third world countries. There are no clear-cut proposals regarding Foreign Direct Investment (FDI) in the Dunkel Draft.

With regard to services, doubts were expressed by Brazil and India, that the third world countries would be swamped by banking and insurance firms from the advanced countries. Also, the LDCs would not be able to contribute much in those services where they have a comparative advantage i.e. those involving labour (like construction, computer programming), since the movement of people across borders will not be permitted. After initial dithering, the possibility of an agreement on services is nevertheless in sight. Rules regarding transparency of regulations, most-favoured nation (MFN) treatment, maintenance of safeguards and liberalisation in stages will apply uniformly to all kinds of services, including labour-related services.

11.3 Intellectual Property Rights

We next come to TRIPS (Trade Related Intellectual Property Rights) where the Dunkel Proposals demand a lot of changes in intellectual property protection from India and other third world countries. TRIPS is an area where the Dunkel proposals demand most concessions from India, which recognises only process patents not product patents for pharmaceutical and agricultural products, and limits patents to 14 years or 7 years from the time the patent was applied for. India would also have liked to retain flexibility for excluding vital areas like pharmaceuticals, chemicals and food technology from product patents. The Dunkel proposals require tougher enforcement of copyrights and trade marks by India. It requires a change in Indian legislation on patents to make it conform to the Paris Convention. Apart from animal varieties, plant varieties and biological processes, product patents have immediately to be granted in all other areas. In so far as only process patents continue during a transitional period, the burden of proof will be reversed and placed on the defendant. The term of the patents will be increased to 20 years. Assuming that the Uruguay round agreement enters into force in 1993, India would have till 2003 to change the relevant legislation.

Intellectual Property and its protection is the most

contentious issue in the Uruguay round human being is gifted with the quality of thinking and is forever trying to find solutions to problems. New ideas and inventions keep on emerging in science and technology. Similarly, new creations are made in the field of art and literature. All this is the outcome of human intelligence. The resulting outcome is known as intellectual property. Intellectual property is thus the creation of the human mind, the human intellect. Intellectual property is created by incorporating information in tangible objects capable of being multiplied an unlimited number of times anywhere in the world. The property is basically in the concept, incorporated in an actual product or process. Intellectual property is usually divided into two branches, (1) Patents, Designs and Trade marks, which are also termed 'industrial property' and (2) copyrights. It is customary to distinguish between inventions that consist of products, and inventions that consist of processes. There may also be a combination of both. Thus there could be a product patent, a process patent or a product and process patent. A new process or an improved process could be a good subject matter for a patent; however to be patentable a process must lead to some result.

India is governed by the Indian Patents Act of 1970. If this is altered in consonance with the Paris Convention the nascent indigenous pharmaceutical industry will be destroyed; research efforts in process development would be dampened and drug prices would be pushed up enormously. Let it be noted that nations which signed the Paris Convention in the last century were all Western nations. The period when the convention was signed saw a spate of inventions in a variety of fields in Europe. The Berne Convention was for protecting copyrights of authors, and artists while the Paris Convention dealt with wider issues.

Negotiations on TRIPS began in March 1987. Developed countries, by and large, have supported a comprehensive package on TRIPS. This package would be under GATT and would encompass substantive standards of protection for all areas of intellectual property (patents, trademarks, copyrights), effective enforcement measures (both at the border and internally) and effective dispute settlement provisions. In addition to a draft legal text submitted by the USA, other legal texts also have been submitted by the EC, Switzerland and Japan. Most developed countries desire a straight-forward application of GATT to the standards for copyright protection set out in the Berne Convention for the Protection of Literary and Artistic Works.

The polarization of views between developed and developing countries is sharper. The popular impression of TRIPS in developed countries is that it is all a matter of piracy and counterfeiting. But there is more to TRIPS than that. LDCs are genuinely concerned about patent protection for technologically sophisticated but vitally important goods like drugs, chemical fertilizers, and plant hybrids. LDCs have major technological and public interest objectives to consider. India would like to retain the flexibility for excluding vital areas like pharmaceuticals, plant hybrids and food technology from product patents. The patent system is also important for promoting industrial development, as is the mechanism of compulsory licensing of a new product. Besides, India and 14 other LDCs feel that GATT involvement should be limited to broader measures to address copyright piracy and trademark counterfeiting. There should be flexibility in national laws on TRIPS in accordance with developmental objectives. Apart from piracy and counterfeiting, guidelines in other areas like substantive standards should be administered outside GATT, possibly through the World Intellectual Property Organization (WIPO).

11.4 Indian Position on GATT

The political leadership in India will have to firm up its views on matters of vital interest to India like TRIPS, textiles and agriculture, before the final negotiations resume in Geneva in December 1993.

India will seek changes in the Dunkel Draft in five key areas. These are: (1) Trade in textiles, (2) Agricultural trade liberalisation, (3) Rules governing anti-dumping, (4) Provisions on cross-retaliation, and (5) TRIPS.

Commerce ministry officials say that the patent stalemate in multi-lateral talks, owing to differences between leading industrialized nations on agricultural trade liberalisation has allowed India the necessary time to evolve its own stand. At the same time the government is keen on an early conclusion to the Uruguay Round of negotiations. For India has a high stake in the finalisation of a new multi-lateral trade Agreement. The collapse of the round would only lead to the growth of protectionism in the industrialised countries, through the strengthening of regional trade blocks, to the detriment of LDCs like India.

In textiles, the improvements in the draft agreement that India will seek are a shorter period than 10 years, prescribed by Dunkel for phasing out protectionist MFA, and faster integration of the textile trade with the GATT framework by removing quota restrictions on a large number of items in the very initial years.

India seeks seven specific improvements in the Dunkel proposals regarding agricultural trade liberalisation. These are:

1. Exemption from a commitment on reduction of subsidy on purchase of food in order to ensure food security. This means that India can continue to subsidise its buffer stock operations;
2. Enhancement for LDCs of the maximum percentage of subsidies for agricultural commodities from the 10 percent provided in the text, implying that agricultural subsidies can cross the ten- percent ceiling to reasonable limits;
3. exemption of input subsidies from the maximum limits prescribed for Indian farmers(at least those owning up to four hectares) for the purpose of calculating the aggregate measure of support (AMS);

4. Additional flexibility in regard to subsidies to crops grown on marginal land, implying special provisions for less productive agricultural land;
5. Adoption of a realistic period for enforcement of external price comparisons;
6. An exemption for LDCs from ratification in respect of some basic food stuffs even after balance of payment problems are over to safeguard against pronounced fluctuations;
7. Sharper reduction in export subsidy doled out to their farmers by developed countries, to protect interests of developing country farmers.

In the area of anti-dumping rules, India would like to press for the following provisions:

1. A threshold to be fixed for market penetration by the products of a country before anti-dumping duties can be levied against it;
2. A level of sales in the domestic market of the developing country which is considered adequate for the purpose of making price comparisons;
3. Immunity from anti-dumping investigations to suppliers who are already subject to quantitative restrictions;
4. A "Sunset" clause for anti-dumping action so that protection for sunset industries in the developed countries is not provided.

A declaration from the developed countries that take recourse to cross-retaliation against LDCs only when the adverse effect of dumping or other violation is very great and a clear commitment on the repeal of domestic laws which authorise unilateral retaliation for economic reasons, are the two other improvements sought by India.

With regard to the Dunkel proposals on TRIPS, which have been the most controversial of all, the government will try to secure the following improvements:

1. A special compulsory licensing provision for food products and pharmaceuticals;

2. A clear commitment that imports will not be regarded as a "working" of the patents;
3. Special provisions recognising the primacy of public interest in LDCs with regard to patent protection; and
4. Adequate safeguards for farmers against plant breeder's rights.

There has been very little difference of opinion on legal consequences of an acceptance of the Dunkel Text. The general opinion is that the Indian patent law would have to be overhauled. The difference of opinion is on the assessment of the economic implications of such a move.

One view is that the general level of prices of all medicines would increase five to ten times. However, the present estimate of the number of drugs sold in the country which are under patents is 15 percent. Most medicines which are widely used are not protected according to official sources. Such medicines should be unaffected.

Commerce ministry officials feel that it would be difficult to fix a term of patent protection on the basis of national criteria; and the period of 20 years has to be viewed against the background of the fact that it has international consensus. Also, in the case of drugs, it takes about eight to ten years to get marketing approval after the grant of a patent. On the other hand, some studies have shown that global trade could gain up to US$ 120 billion a year with a successful GATT agreement and all would benefit from this.

Again, the current draft agreement has many useful rules for the settlement of international trade disputes, protectionist use of technical standards, anti-dumping measures, countervailing duties and numerous other non-tariff barriers to trade. It also offers safeguards for intellectual property, which remains a subject of controversy in India, but which is perhaps the only way now left for India, to avert protracted and damaging international disputes over intellectual property rights.

11.5 Third World Perspectives

The absence of a global agreement on trade could mean each country, or group of countries would go their own way, most likely generating fierce competition and world wide disputes over trade. A country like India, on the verge of joining the global economy in a meaningful way, would probably find access to world markets very difficult without the help of GATT.

The US administration has congressional sanction under a special fast track legislation, by which international agreements can be negotiated without detailed congressional surveillance, only up to 1993 to clinch international trade deals. After that, the American legislature may re-open the whole issue for domestic debate.

It is maintained in India that the multilateral trading system sanctioned by GATT was status quoits, maintaining the predominance and pre-eminence of the first world countries on the international economy. Hardly any efforts have been made to lessen the first world and the third world. The negotiations and discussions were all first world oriented. Thus GATT has not taken into account the pivotal role-played by MNCs in fostering the inequitable relations between the first and the third world. Thus, while the clauses dealing with trade and development remained on the agenda of successive rounds of negotiations, the constraints in meeting the requirements of GATT arising from the exploitation of the third world by MNCs, did not come in for consideration, let alone discussion, even in the Uruguay Round. Now on the contrary, paradoxically the issue under consideration is how to provide greater strength to the MNCs for exploiting third world market.

If the proposals in the Dunkel Draft on the new patent regime were accepted, there would be a serious impact on the availability of new products through ingenious efforts, on the prices of new products, which would be exorbitant. In particular, the consumer would suffer, as high prices would have to be paid for essential medicines. R and D activity would also be seriously jeopardised. The product patent regime will take away opportunities for developing innovative processes. Small and tiny enterprises may have to close down, and thus employment prospects will be jeopardised in the third world.

On the other hand, some maintain that the absence of product patents really kills serious research into new products in India. Companies prefer to take the easy way of making some small changes in the process. Thus, Indian creativity is crippled. Besides, a weak patent law takes away the monetary incentive to spend money on serious R and D since the product can easily be copied.

The TRIMS proposals will have adverse effects on opportunities for domestic industry. Foreign investors would be able to decide the level and extent of foreign equity holdings and also the industries in which they should invest, which would naturally be in consumer durables and simple technologies, yielding huge profits. Domestic industry will thus be seriously affected. At the same time, one must also remember that India cannot do without new technology and investment from abroad.

Subsidies will be reduced for agricultural products, cutting them down to 10 percent of the cost of production. This will have a deleterious impact on farmers. The PDS (Public Distribution System) will also have to be remodelled and revamped. There will be extensive intervention in the third world's policies for independent agricultural development. However, sooner or later agriculture would have to do without subsidies and all would then benefit.

If the services sector and banking and insurance are kept open to foreign financial institutions, savings will be diverted to foreign institutions. The weaker sections of society in the third world countries will be the worst sufferers in this dispensation. While this may be true, it is also true that the only way to improve the gross inefficiency of public sector financial institutions is to make them face competition from

Indian and foreign companies, Any improvement in the functioning of public sector banks will have a multiplier effect on the whole of Indian business.

The third world countries by compromising in the GATT would have to face the combined pressure of the world's wealthiest and most powerful countries. The alternative is for a country to isolate itself. The "New World Order" has ominous implications for trade issues as well. Thus Uruguay Round has crucial implications for the Third World.

11.6 Options for India

With around 40 percent of India's exports being accounted for by the United States and Europe, any denial of access to these two markets could result in a quick return to the near bankrupt balance of payments situation of 1991. And those, who believe that such considerations have little to do with farmers, will do well to remember that agricultural exports will also be hit, and so will the import of several commodities, including petroleum products, which are critical to the rural sector.

The benefits for India of the Dunkel Draft are most visible in the case of the country's textile exports. Textile exports so far were managed by the multi fibre agreement (MFA) since 1974. The MFA expired in 1992, and there will be a phasing out of the MFA over a ten-year period. However, the definition of textiles has been enlarged, so that products not currently restrained will also come under the ambit of liberalisation. There was very little 'actual' liberalisation till 2000. Most of the liberalisation came subsequently.

The emphasis on increasing market access, for instance, has been interpreted primarily as an instrument to prise open the Indian market. But it also helps Indian exporters gain access to more lucrative markets than the Indian one.

And with a growing recognition that sustained growth in Indian agriculture will require increased farm exports, the Dunkel Draft may not as adversely affect farmers as the more militant farmers' associations would have us to believe.

Such benefits will have to be weighed against the costs of the Dunkel Draft. There has been considerable attention drawn to the adverse consequences of patenting plant varieties not just in immediate economic terms, but also in terms of its impact, in the long run, on the genetic resources of the Third World.

If the rejection of the Dunkel Draft is not a valid option, all that can be sought is that as many favourable changes as possible are incorporated in a final agreement, if and when one does come about.

And India cannot hope for too many such changes either. Its negotiating strength has been reduced by the developing world being far less of a force today that it was when the Uruguay Round began in Punta del Este. Moreover, with wide divergences among developing countries, India cannot expect to benefit from the regionalisation of world trade.

There has been very little debate on the specifics of the government's negotiating position on the Dunkel Draft. Indeed; the focus on the impossible demand for rejecting the entire draft has contributed to the governments' negotiating position being determined primarily by short-term considerations.

The current political uncertainty is also bound to make the government more concerned with the immediate impact of a trade agreement rather than the costs of opting out, which will only become evident in the long-term. The less than comfortable balance of payments position is also likely to keep the focus on the short-term effects on trade.

In an atmosphere, where political attention is focused on non-economic issues, the chances of the negotiating position being determined by a bureaucratic problem solving approach, rather than a long-term vision, is even greater. It is thus; hardly surprising that official concern has been almost entirely concentrated on the impact on textiles and pharmaceuticals, both areas, where the Dunkel Draft can have an immediate effect.

In case the Government cannot get the developed countries to accept our demand for the exclusion of chemical products from the scope of patentability, then we must provide for the license of right, a form of compulsory license to manufacture, which alone give full scope to the manufacturers to produce patented inventions after paying royalties to the patent holder. Without such a provision, the government would not be able to ensure the development of strong national companies and also keep the prices of drugs down.

Unfortunately, the government is willing to jettison this provision and is searching for a way out in the provision for compulsory licensing for non-commercial public use. It is not difficult to see that this cannot cover many products. Non-commercial public use implies production at government cost. Clearly, in India where health care is now largely in the private sector, the provision for non-commercial public use cannot cover many patented drugs.

The claim that by using price control mechanisms the government will be able to make drugs available at cheap prices is also based on false premise. Thanks to import being treated as 'working' of the patent under the TRIPS agreement, most drugs will be imported from the patent holders who, in the absence of competition, will be free to charge monopoly prices. Only in those cases where the patent holder has established local production will the government be able to intervene and regulate prices.

Similarly, the attention of the public is being diverted from the real issues as far as seeds are concerned. The attempt of the Ministry of Commerce has been to keep some ill-informed criticisms alive by reiterating that the government will not accept the patenting of seeds or the removal of the right of farmers to save seed. In fact close reading of the Dunkel Draft, shows that the right of farmers to save seeds was not threatened by the Dunkel Proposals. Therefore, no brave fight is required to get the US to give assurances on the right of farmers to save seed.

However, the view that the failure of the Uruguay Round will have disastrous consequences for India is unduly pessimistic. Trade wars will not be a necessary consequence of failure of the Uruguay Round, since both the GATT Treaty and organisation will continue under the provisions of the Tokyo Round, howsoever frayed it might have become. Trade anarchy is thus not inevitable catastrophic prognosis is therefore uncalled for.

The Dunkel proposals can by no means be described as uniformly advantageous to India. On the contrary; there are elements within them, which may have an adverse impact on Indian commerce. A comparison of the gains and losses if India signs the Dunkel Draft is called for. The Dunkel Draft should not be a 'take it' or 'leave it' agreement and India should sign the Draft only after its reservations are considered and hopefully incorporated.

11.7 GATT and WTO

For several decades, GATT (General Agreement on Tariffs and Trade) was applied on a provisional basis. It was a multilateral agreement containing rules relative to trade in goods, and although it operated like a permanent agreement, it was without a permanent institutional framework, and was serviced by an ad hoc secretariat. The WTO now provides a permanent institutional framework for the multilateral trading system, with its own secretariat. In addition the WTO not only covers trade in goods, as the GATT rules did, but also trade in services, and trade-related aspects of IPRs (Intellectual Property Rights). Also, the dispute settlement mechanism has been considerably strengthened in the WTO.

In the preamble of the Marrakesh Agreement establishing the WTO, the parties to the agreement recognize certain objectives to which they wish to contribute through the multilateral trading system. It is recognized that Member's relations in the field of trade and economic endeavour, should be conducted with a view to raising standards of living, ensuring full employment and a large and steadily growing volume of real income, and effective demand and expanding the production of and trade in goods and services, while allowing for the optimal use of the world's resources in accordance with the objectives of sustainable development. The WTO agreement also recognizes the need for "positive efforts" to ensure that LDCs and especially the least developed among them, secure a share in the growth in international trade commensurate with the needs of their economic development.

The main functions of the WTO are:

1. To administrator WTO trade agreements.
2. To provide a forum for trade negotiations.
3. To handle trade disputes.
4. To monitor national trade policies.
5. To provide technical assistance and training for LDCs.
6. To cooperate with other international organizations.

11.8 WTO–GATT Rounds and Ministerial Conferences

During the period, 1947 to 2009, the contracting parties successfully concluded eight rounds of trade negations and seven Ministerial Conferences. These eight rounds and seven ministerial conferences are listed below, with the years in which they were held.

- 1947–The birth of General Agreement on Tariffs and Trade (GATT). The GATT was signed by 23 countries. The agreement contained tariff concessions agreed during the first multilateral trade negotiations, and a set of rules designed to prevent these concessions from being frustrated by restrictive trade measures.
- 1949–Second Round at Annecy France. The contracting parties exchanged some 5,000 tariff concessions.
- 1950-51–Third Round at Torque, U.K. The contracting parties exchanged some 8,700 tariff concessions, yielding tariff reductions of about 25 percent in relation to the 1948 level.

- 1956–Fourth Round at Geneva. The round produced 82.5 billion worth of tariff reductions.
- 1960-62–Dillon Round. Named in honour of the U.S. Under–Secretary of State, Douglas Dillon, who proposed the negotiations, the fifth Round was divided into two phases. The first was concerned with negotiations, which resulted in about 4,400 tariff concessions covering US$ 4.49 billion of trade.
- 1964-67–Kennedy Round. For the first time, negotiations departed from product by product approach, to an across the board of linear method of cutting tariffs for industrial goods. The working hypothesis of a 50 percent target cut in tariff level was achieved in many areas. Concessions covered an estimated total value of trade of about US$ 40 billion.
- 1973-79-Tokyo Round. Launched in the Japanese capital, the seventh round resulted in tariff reductions and bindings, covering more than US$ 300 billion of trade. As a result the weighted average tariffs on manufactured goods in the world's nine major industrial markets declined from 7.0 percent to 4.0 percent. Agreements were reached on subsidies and counter veiling measures, technical barriers to trade, import licensing procedures, government procurement, customs valuation, a revised anti-dumping code, and trade in bovine meat, diary products and civil aircraft.
- 1986-94–Uruguay Round. It was the result of the most comprehensive trade negotiations ever undertaken including average tariff cuts of 40 percent on industrial products, average increase of tariff binding from 21 percent to 73 percent for LDCs, from 78 percent to 99 percent for developed countries and from 73 percent to 98 percent for transitional economies, a comprehensive programme of agricultural reform, phase out of quantitative restrictions on textiles and clothing, new agreements on trade and services, intellectual property

rights, sanitary and phytosanitory measures, new sources and trade related investment measures, and strengthened agreements on safeguards, technical barriers, customs valuation, import licensing, state trading subsidies and anti-dumping measures. The Round also strengthened the dispute settlement system and created the WTO.

- 1996–First Ministerial Conference (Singapore). The purpose of this First Conference was to examine issues related to the work of the WTO's first two years of activity and the implementation of the Uruguay Round Agreements. Other agendas included-assessing the implementation of commitments under the WTO Agreements and decisions; reviewing the ongoing negotiations and work programme; examine developments in world trade; and address the challenges of an evolving world economy.
- 1998–Second Ministerial Conference (Geneva). The crucial importance of the multilateral rule-based trading system was discussed; concerns over the marginalization of least-developed countries and certain small economies was highlighted and five new countries viz., Congo, Democratic Republic of Congo, Mongolia, Niger and Panama joined the WTO.
- 1999–Third Ministerial Conference (Seattle). This Conference aimed at launching major new negotiations to further liberalize international trade and to review some current trade rules, specifically pertaining to agreements on services (the General Agreement on Trade in Services, GATS). There were proposals for the Seattle meeting to produce a special deal to help least-developed countries gain easier access to richer countries' markets, and to develop further work on technical assistance to least-developed countries.
- 2001–Fourth Ministerial Conference (Doha). The focus of the Conference included, (a) specific initiatives to assist least-developed countries (LDCs), including a call for

greater market access; (b) A special mechanism for discussing and negotiating implementation issues; (c) A comprehensive examination of technical cooperation and capacity building activities, and (d) Procedures for ensuring more active and effective participation of all member governments in the WTO.

- 2003–Fifth Ministerial Conference (Cancun). This Ministerial Conference marked an important stop on the road to completing the Doha Development Agenda (DDA) round of trade negotiations. Prominent issues discussed included agreement on the modalities, or framework, for negotiations on issues of investment, competition, transparency in government procurement and trade facilitation.
- 2005–Sixth Ministerial Conference (Hong Kong). The main aim of the Conference was to settle a range of questions that will shape the final agreement of the Doha Development Agenda. Agreement on formulas and other details that will determine the scale of reductions in tariffs on thousands of products and on farm subsidies and negotiations in services and other development issues were highly on the agenda.
- 2009–Seventh Ministerial Conference (Geneva). LDC-specific issues were underlined as needing particular attention, including Duty-Free Quota-Free market access, cotton, and the LDC Waiver for Services. The particular needs of Small and Vulnerable Economies were also emphasized. There was broad agreement that the growing number of bilateral and regional trade agreements is an issue for the multilateral trading system, and that there is a need to ensure that the two approaches to trade opening continue to complement each other. There was strong convergence on the importance of accessions in broadening and strengthening the WTO and on the importance of technical assistance at all stages of the accession process.

11.9 WTO Agreement

The agreement establishing WTO is called the WTO Agreement. It is the legal instrument through which all countries participating in the Uruguay Round decided to create the WTO. The WTO Agreement includes provisions on establishment, scope, functions and structure, relations with other organizations, secretariat, budget and contributions, legal status, decision-making procedures, including special voting procedures, amendment, and definition of original members, accession, non-application, and acceptance, entry into force and deposit mobilization and final provisions. Since all the other agreements are annexed to the agreement establishing the WTO, the expression "the WTO Agreement" is understood to cover the totality of all the agreements.

11.10 WTO: Sub-clauses of Agreement

The WTO's agreements are often called the Final Act of the 1986-1994 Uruguay Round of trade negotiations. This is a summary of the Agreements.

1. Agreement on Agriculture (AoA).
2. Agreement on Sanitary and Phytosanitory Measures.
3. Agreement on Textiles and clothing.
4. Agreement on Technical Barriers to Trade (TBT).
5. Agreement on Trade-related Aspects of Investment Measures (TRIMS).
6. Agreement on Implementation of Article VI (Anti-Dumping).
7. Agreement on Implementation of Article VII (Customs Valuation).
8. Agreement on Pre-shipment Inspection (PSI).
9. Agreement on Rules of origin.
10. Agreement on Subsidies and Countervailing Measures.
11. Agreement on Safeguards.
12. General Agreement on Trade in Services.
13. Agreement on Trade Related Aspects of Intellectual Property Rights (TRIPs), including trade in counterfeit goods.

11.11 India and the WTO

India is a founding member of the GATT (1947). It actively participated in the Uruguay Round of Negotiations. India strongly favours the multilateral approach to trade relations and grants MFN (Most Favoured Nation) treatment to all its trading partners, including some who are not members of WTO. India has participated actively in all the Ministerial Conferences held under WTO auspices. India is committed to ensure that the sectors in which the LDCs enjoy a comparative advantage are adequately opened up to international trade, and also that the special and differential treatment provisions for LDCs under the different WTO Agreements are translated into specific enforceable dispensations, in order that LDCs are facilitated in their developmental efforts. India feels that the multilateral system would itself gain if it adequately reflected these concerns of the LDCs, so as to create the necessary impetus to enable developing country members to catch up with their developed country counterparts.

Under the Uruguay Round, India has bound 67 percent of all its tariff lines, whereas prior to that only 6 percent of tariff levies were bound. The bindings range from 0 percent to 300 percent for agricultural products and from 0 percent to 40 percent for other products. Under the Uruguay Round, manufactured products were bound at 25 percent on intermediate goods, and 40 percent on finished goods. The phased reduction to these bound levels from the very high levels prevailing in 1990 is where necessary, in instalments over the period 1995 to 2005. In textiles where reductions will be achieved over ten years, India has reserved the right to duty levels prevailing in 1990, if the integration process envisaged under the Agreement on Textiles and Clothing does not materialize in full or is delayed. Finally, in agriculture, except for a few goods, India's bound rates range from 100 percent to 300 percent. India is in the process of re-negotiating some of its tariff bindings. Many applied tariffs are below the Uruguay Round level.

12

India and the European Union (EU): Shared Values and Future Directions

---

12.1 EU: World's Most Successful Regional Organization

The European Union (EU) today is the world's most successful regional organization, accounting for 63 percent of total bloc exports. Intra-bloc exports in SAARC, (South Asia Association for Regional Cooperation) with India as a member, are still only 5 percent. The EU has shown much more commitment than any other regional organization. It has aspects of both supra-nationalism and inter-governmentalism. India also has many similarities with EU. EU's development has transformed governance in Europe, influencing everything from regulations on the habitat of birds, to voting in WTO. It has also altered global politics, governance and the relationship of nation-states in the post-cold war era. There is nevertheless a "democratic deficit" in Europe. Decisions are made by governmental leaders and bureaucrats without direct input from voters. In India too "democracy" means periodic elections, which bring about a "compromise between competing elites", and without altering the basic conditions of the poverty-ridden masses.

12.2 India-EU Relations

India and the EU are the two largest democracies in the world, sharing a common bond of pluralism, consultation, consensus, and rule of law, strength of democratic institutions, a strong and free press, and an independent judiciary. These are the principal features defining their strategic partnership. These principles help manage their continental-sized polities and economies. Decision-making structures are federative, inclusive, caring and conciliatory.

India and the EU are the foremost examples of multiculturalism, that countries elsewhere in the world must embrace as an inevitable consequences of globalization, and the new world order. India views the EU as an independent and indispensable pillar of a world edifice resting on multiple pillars, capable of making significant contributions towards fostering a rule-based international order, and in coming to terms with the challenges of managing global interdependence. The EU is India's largest trading partner, and source of Foreign Direct Investment (FDI). Our economic partnership is based on firm foundations. Indian companies are investing in sectors as diverse as IT (Information Technology), bio-technology, food-processing, automotive components, and pharmaceuticals.

India sees the EU as a natural partner in its economic development, and interaction with the rest of the world. The strategic partnership is no longer economic-driven, but covers diverse areas of engagement. We share a mutuality of interests on many global issues. We are partners in an intensified fight against terrorism, nuclear proliferation, unsustainable-environment, and sectarian conflict. When the EU the world's biggest trading bloc and the largest integrated single market economy co-operates with India–the second most populous nation and the fourth largest, fast growing economy, the significance of the partnership goes beyond bilateral relations and impacts on global equations.

The EU sees Indian multiculturalism and its apparent success, as an example where one can learn from each other's experience. In EU circles it is felt if India can exist as a mosaic of ethnicities, religions, languages and cultures, why can't Europe follow the same path?

At the superficial level, there are plenty of similarities between the EU and India. The EU comprises 27 nations with more queuing up. India has 28 states, each marked by distinctive culture, and 18 official languages. Christianity is the primary religion in Europe: Hinduism in India. Both EU and India have significant minority populations. But, of course, there are profound differences too. Europe after all is the cradle of modern nationalism, and some members of the EU are the oldest nation-states in the world. Thus, however much the EU tries to gloss over angularities of nationalism; it continues to stumble on them.

What the claim to equate EU with India does is to posit civilizational basis for Europe. The problem with this formulation came to the fore when both France and the Netherlands rejected the European constitution. An important reason for this is strong nationalist sentiments in both countries, as opposed to pan-European identities. The attitude to particular religious minority-Muslims in Europe brings to the fore EU's policy of multicultural harmonization. As a greater number of Muslims, many of them belonging to a generation raised and nurtured in Europe are implicated in terrorist acts. EU member-states policies towards minorities and migration are being severely tested. The role of the State should be clearly defined-does the State impose hard secularism and uniform citizenship on its citizens as in France, or does it give more play to multiple notions of identity? Many of these concerns, especially with regard to EU' expansion plans come into focus when the question of Turkey's entry to the EU crops up.

India's problems are similar to EU's in many aspects. Despite the success of India's Multiculturalism, there are serious flaws in the ways it is formulated and practised in India. Though the Indian State has been vociferous in its defence of multiculturalism, it has often failed to deliver. The Constitution of India has clauses that contain aspects of Hindu majoritarianism, despite India's professed multiculturalism, and secular credentials. The State's and Judiciary's construction of Hinduism is intent on homogeneity. The wording of the Constitution is also instructive. The reference to Hindus in Article 25 includes Sikhs, Jains and Buddhists. It is not only the State that makes a mockery of the slogan-

"Unity in Diversity". For most Indians, diversity is something that is best celebrated in theory. As soon as diversity threatens the majority, it falls back on uniformity and national unity, for "survival of the Nation".

Economic co-operation between India and Europe is gathering momentum. EU-India trade has grown impressively and doubled from €28.6 billion in 2003 to over € 55billion in 2007. EU investment to India has more than tripled since 2003 from €759 million to €2.4 billion in 2006 and trade in commercial services has more than doubled from €5.2 billion in 2002 to €12.2 billion in 2006. EU is a major source of high grade technology and technology transfer. Indo-German collaboration companies were market leaders in as many as 15 product groups.

As economic growth in the EU is projected to rebound in the coming years, this is the appropriate time to give a boost to India-EU economic cooperation. Indo-EU ties are now upgraded to a "strategic partnership", after the annual summits since 2000, covering all aspects of economic and political cooperation.

Movement of professionals between EU and India should be possible with the mutual recognition of higher qualifications. With a special relationship, Indian companies can penetrate in a big way rapidly growing European outsourcing. Integration of economies would improve the competitiveness of both India and the EU.

A rapidly aging population coupled with increasingly better standards of living amongst EU citizens has prompted the EU to look towards Asia to bridge labour-supply gaps.

Europe is today a global super power of world historical importance, second to none in economic clout. It has constructed one of the most successful systems of government – the modern social welfare state, which for all its flaws has brought in unprecedented prosperity and security to Europe's people. It is the single most successful contributor to voluntary international cooperation. The original European Economic

Community (ECC) of 1957 has grown from the founding six members to 27, knitting together 500 million people. Its values are spreading across the globe–far more attractive, in many respects, than those of America.

Europe's trajectory is up, not down, and is even rising. Northern Europe's social democracies are on top of the World Economic Forum's ranking of the most competitive economies. 60 percent of US foreign investment goes to Europe.

US business invests more in European nations like Belgium, Ireland, and Switzerland than in the whole of China or India. Instruments to engineer peace, the softer tools of civilian power, lie with Europe–The "quiet super power".

EU has emerged as Europe's most innovative and significant contribution to modernity. Europe and EU emphasizes community relationships over individual autonomy, cultural diversity over assimilation, quality of life over accumulation of wealth, sustainable development over unlimited material growth, deep play over unrelenting toil, and universal human rights, India too values all these qualities. Hence we should work together harmonize our synergies, through closer collaboration and interaction.

It is only through multiculturalism shared by both India and the EU that global problems such as terrorism, environmental degradation, reviving WTO talks and religious fundamentalism can be mitigated.

The Berlin Declaration, commemorating EU at 50, states "for centuries Europe has been an idea, holding out hope of peace and understanding. That hope has been fulfilled". The real success of both India and the EU are linguistic pluralism, accommodation of diversities and heterogeneities and above all functioning vibrant parliamentary democracies.

The commonality of values between India and the EU pluralism, consultation, strength of democratic institutions, independent judiciary and free press, are part of the mutuality of interests. India and the European Union are the two foremost examples of multiculturalism and plurality of identities, something that countries in other continents must embrace as an inevitable aspects and consequence of globalization. Despite the flaws of multiculturalism, India and the EU see each other as indispensable pillars, making significant contributions towards fostering a rule-based international order and in meeting the challenges of global reciprocity and independence.

The forerunner of the European Union (EU) was the European Coal and Steel Community, established in the early 1950s. This evolved into the European Economic Community (EEC) also known as the European Common Market (ECM) or the European Community (EC), and now as the European Union (EU). It is the most successful of regional economic integration schemes.

The EEC, originally comprised six nations–Belgium, France, Federal Republic of Germany, Italy, Luxembourg and the Netherlands – came into being on January 1, 1958 by the virtue of the Treaty of Rome of 1957. The EEC was expanded in 1973, with the inclusion of the UK, Denmark and Ireland. Greece joined the community in 1981, Spain and Portugal became members in 1986. Austria, Finland and Sweden also joined the EC later the membership rising to 15. Today the EU has 27 members, including some countries, of the former Soviet Bloc in Eastern Europe, and some of the newly liberated countries of the former Soviet Union.

The objectives of the formation of the EU as envisaged in the Treaty of Rome are:

- Elimination of tariffs, quotas and other barriers on intra – community trade,
- Having a common internal tariff on imports from the rest of the World,
- Allowing the free movement of factors of production within the community,
- Harmonizing of taxation and monetary policies, and also social security policies, and

- Adopting a common policy on agriculture, transport and competition in industry.

12.3 Indo-EU Trade

The EU, taken as a single unit is India's largest trading partner. India's main exports to the EU include textiles, jute, leather and leather goods, and polished diamonds engineering goods, chemicals, and marine products. Imports include edible oils, fertilizers, dairy products, steel, capital goods, optical instruments, alumina and copper products, synthetic rubber, photo and cinema equipment. India also receives technology investment and development from the EU countries.

India's export performance to EU has been rather poor. Lack of price competitiveness, poor quality, poor reputation with respect to delivery schedules, inadequate export marketing skills, and protectionist policies of the EU countries, are the main factors for a sluggish growth in India-EU trade, particularly India's exports to EU. India should pay great attention to the emerging opportunities in the EU, and improve quality of exports and stick to delivery schedules.

13

Resurgent India: Forging Ahead

13.1 Commitment to Democracy

A firm commitment to democracy advances in technology, health, education and the economy, teamed with a new mindset is helping India make its mark in the global arena in a big way. What has probably changed, more than anything else, is the attitude. Indians are demanding their place in the sun. They refuse to be dismissed as citizens of just another "developing nation", an epithet used for all countries that do not match up to Western standards of development. In fact more than what the government has achieved, Indians have pushed the country way up in the global arena. India is being talked about as the next Asian superpower, along with China. Illiteracy, population, and poverty still haunt Indians-but, there are areas in which the country is definitely shining. India's growth rate and its achievements may be far greater, because it is accompanied by a healthy democratic system. In fact, literacy rates have moved up almost 65 percent in 2009 from a meagre 48 percent, a decade back. Our higher education system is lauded across the world. Indians are considered "big players" in software development. A self-confident resurgent India is embracing its role as an Asian superpower.

13.2 Technology Upgradation

Technology has touched more lives than we can imagine. Farmers in Punjab, to matchmakers in Mumbai, everyone uses internet, to check everything from weather reports to appropriate alliances. India's national highways are getting even better using the latest technologies. More than economics, what has changed is Indians confidence in themselves. Indians are no longer apologetic about working hard and making money. Affluence and money are no longer looked down upon-why we even have celebrity Chefs! Several young people prefer to turn entrepreneurs, than depend on jobs that are hard to come by.

To succeed in today's India, you do not need a legacy of wealth or connections. It is knowledge-based competence on show, not only in information technology, but across a broad spectrum of activities, including cinema, art, literature, sports and fine arts. That a nation of a billion people, ranging from the super-rich to the abysmally poor, continue to practice what is the world's most open system of government, is nothing short of a miracle.

13.3 Reorientation of the Role of State

With the transformation from a planned economy to a market economy, not just economic institutions, but a drastic reorientation of the role of the State takes place as well.

In Western Europe, the Mercantilist State was openly interventionist-its goal was not the maximization of welfare, but the increase of State power as well. International trade was an extension of domestic trade, and as an adjunct to its capacity to wage war. Exports were encouraged, imports curbed and gold thus obtained was used as settlement to finance a professional army and navy. The market regulated itself, and the State had minimalist functions in the post industrial revolution.

Socialist economies redefined the goals of the State, from Statism to Capitalism. A "Statist" economic system is one oriented towards maximizing state power, while in a capitalist system maximizing profit is the prime objective. The Soviet Union proved to be a classic case of a Statist economy.

In Statist economies, every major interaction between economic agents is mediated to a greater or lesser extent by the State. This makes decision-making lines run vertically instead of horizontally. This is the opposite of a competitive economy, where to ensure maximum speed and flexibility in decision-making, the lines of interaction run horizontally between consumers, intermediaries, and producers, with no interference from the State.

This shift requires:

- Reduction in the role and functions of the State;
- Enforcement of a complex framework of rules and regulations to ensure smooth functioning of the market;
- Enlargement of State functions and therefore its administrative capacity; and
- Synchronization of withdrawal from direct intervention and the development of regulatory functions for a smooth transition.

The transformation from a planned to a market economy does not involve a weakening or withdrawal of the State. On the contrary, it requires a strong state–a state with unquestioned authority to promulgate new laws and considerably enhanced administrative powers to enforce and regulate them.

After a period of glasnost and perestroika, the FSU (former Soviet Union) adopted "shock therapy" in 1992, dismantling centrally directed and planned production. China on the other hand did not follow and ask for IMF/IBRD help. It kept in place central planning and distribution, and only gradually reduced central intervention.

The shift from plan to market without proper institutions in a market-driven world, only weaken the state. China's economic liberalization has reduced the state's share of the output of its *socialist domain*, without being able to tax the newer sectors of the economy. This has resulted in falling revenue to GDP ratios.

Although India has been the slowest in its reforms, and had the fewest structural problems to cope with, the reforms have reduced the tax to GDP ratios only marginally. The State's role has been weakened, as it has been unable to control expenditure-either of its own or those of the state Governments.

13.4 Liberalization All the Way

Liberalization will definitely lead to higher growth in India, and this will bring more resources for the state through greater taxes and duties. If the Government utilises its resources effectively, it can bring dramatic improvements in the lives of common people. Once the Government gets out of the negative job of running and controlling economic activity, and puts its best people in implementing social action and infrastructure, only then will it enhance the quality of life of the worst-off members in society. This is a quiet triumph of democratic capitalism, and it is in the nature of institutions that they are run by modest men.

"The real debate on globalization is ultimately not about efficiency of markets, nor about importance of modern technology. The debate is on "severe asymmetries of power", for which there is much less tolerance now than in the world that emerged at the end of World War-2"-*Amartaya Sen.*

"In the home of the brave, land of the free! I will not be put down by a bourgeoisie" -old American protest song there may or may not be significantly more inequality today, but what is absolutely clear is that people are far less willing to accept massive inequalities now than they were in 1944, when the Breton Woods agreement led to the establishment of the IMF and World Bank. However, Globalization should not mean we end up as a "frog in the well, whose view of the world is confined to that space".

India's achievements in globalization in terms of (a) Openness to trade and (b) foreign investment have been miniscule. India's share in world exports is a miniscule 0.7 percent. Another measure of globalization is a country's participation in international capital flows, and here too, India's share is insignificant. According to *World Investment Report, 2009*, annual FDI inflows into India in 2008 stood at US$ 41.55 billion only in contrast to annual FDI flows across the globe at US$ 1697.35 billion.

The benefits of Globalization are:

1. Death of distance.
2. Services revolution.
3. Mobility of capital.
4. Price reduction.
5. Expanding markets
6. New ideas for unexploited areas
7. Benefits of improved infrastructure.
8. Entrepreneurial efforts towards infrastructure improvement extending a great deal of benefits to consumers like:

- High speed telecom lines.
- Internet gateways
- Innovative services like WAP (Wireless Application Services).

9. Generation of new ideas to be implemented the world over.
10. Outsourcing of business worldwide and back-office operations.

"Globalization should be accepted as an emerging and powerful global reality, which has its own momentum and we as an independent nation should maximize the advantage for our country, and minimize the risks"-*Bimal Jalan*, RBI Governor.

The transition from a closed to a vibrant economy will take time and will not be painless. It requires much greater agility and less tolerance of waste and sloth. We have too much tolerance of waste, non-work and survival of the inefficient and self-seeking today in India than other fast growing countries.

Obstacles to globalization and increased FDI are:

- Ground level hassles.
- Obstructionist Regulatory framework.
- Rigid and inflexible tax and labour laws.
- Inadequate basic infrastructural amenities like transport power and water.

The suspicions about multilateral organizations like WTO,

IBRD, and IMF are ill founded. Multilateral fora and global rules give more of a chance to the weak than bilateral engagement does.

13.5 Success Story of IT Sector

The largest percentage of Indian origin software professionals working in the US come from AP-Synergy between them and their work-places in the US have helped AP make rapid strides in IT and IT-enabled services.

Easier travel and links are helping Indian standards and quality approach international levels. Standards include soft organizational aspects such as reliability and professionalism. Improving standards will allow us to benefit from our lower costs and help us to increase our share in global trade.

Globalization has become a metaphor for the conditioning framework, which shapes and standardizes our choices. It entrenches corporate values at the epicentre of our society, and it does this through the international and national structures, which facilitate the mobility of capital and speculative finance. Globalization provides a view of the world in which the interests of the powerful are defined as necessity, while the demands of the poor appear as greed, which undermines economic success.

The ideology that underpins globalization focuses on trade as the vehicle for improving the conditions of people everywhere. It is an old idea, which sees the increasing integration of international economies as a positive step and one which would inevitably occur, if markets were not unduly hampered by governments. The restructuring associated with globalization doesn't even attempt to promise anything to those traditionally disadvantaged in our society: the unemployed cannot expect jobs, the poor cannot expect prosperity, and women and other disadvantaged people cannot expect equality. India has achieved considerable constitutional success in reconciling varied regional, caste, and linguistic diversities. She is a triumph of multiculturalism with 28 States and 9

Union territories, held together under exceptionally difficult circumstances. Ultimately democracy is the only way out for the world. The rise of neo-European fascism and neo-Nazism is doomed to failure. The forces of liberalization and globalization will bind together, with appropriate safety nets. India is a "Non-Territorial Cultural Nation"-it has always been so. It can never be "conquered" in that sense. India never needed a "functional" State—"A State of India", governing all of it. The "roots of India" draw their sustenance directly from the nutrition provided by the Indian society.

The reform agenda in the next ten years should be:

- Reform rigid labour laws, but take into account the genuine concerns of labour.
- Revitalize agriculture-if necessary a second "Green Revolution". The present agricultural growth rate of 2 percent should increase to at least 4 percent.
- Drastically strengthen rural infrastructure, but also overhaul existing infrastructure.
- Reduce fiscal deficit to manageable limits, and factor in monetization of fiscal deficits in future scenarios.
- Privatize urban infrastructure-but also redeploy and retrain displaced labour in a satisfactory manner.
- Reform the delivery effectiveness of primary education and health care—the schemes in which government still has an important role.
- To achieve increasing success in the knowledge-economy of tomorrow-KPO (Knowledge Process Outsourcing) needs serious country-risk analysis.
- Strengthen and open new channels of employment outside the IT–ITES world. The IT-sector employment presently stands at about 3 million, out of a total workforce of 400 million.
- The risks of the global economy need to be seriously researched and integrated into the "reform" agenda. Crude price increase, threats to global peace and security, evolving neighbourhood scenarios—SAARC, ASEAN-

WTO, have to be well documented.

13.6 India and China

India will continue down the relatively disorderly path of participatory democracy, raucous, contention-prone, often exasperatingly slow and somewhat tardy compared to the tight hand of totalitarian governance, like in China. India will continue to accommodate and absorb several contradictions. In India, unlike in China, the individual can command the State, but money cynically is indifferent to such philosophical or ideological esotericism.

India's breathtaking originality and sophistication has something more profound to offer tom the world than its ability to imitate America's deeply-flawed consumer society.

Indian intellectuals would best serve India's greatness by speaking frankly about the historic tasks and responsibilities that await the country, and disciplining fantasies and delusions lying in her path.

If India can combine its hard and soft powers, it will surely become a "smart power"-it has already passed the test of political participation that China has not. India is also rapidly adapting to a consensual set-up that many foreigners find attractive. Despite its flaws, it is a safe bet that India is a "smart power of the future".

To succeed in today's India, one does not need a legacy of wealth or connections. Its knowledge-based competence is on show-not only in Information Technology, but across a broad spectrum of activities, including the arts. That a nation of more than a billion people, ranging from the super-rich to the abysmally poor, continue to practice what may be the world's most open system of government is nothing less than a miracle. India's greatest achievement is remaining a vibrant democracy, under exceptionally difficult circumstances.

Appendix

Appendix

Regional Trade Agreements (RTAs) of India at a Glance

Prior to economic reforms process initiated in 1991, India had adopted a very cautious and guarded approach to regionalism. Recognising that RTAs would continue to feature prominently in world trade, India engaged with its trading partners/blocks with the intention of expanding its export market and began concluding in principle agreements and moving in some cases even towards Comprehensive Economic Cooperation Agreements (CECAs) which covers Free Trade Agreement (FTA) in goods, services, investments and identified areas of economic cooperation.

RTAs are an integral part of India's foreign trade policy, complementing the multilateral trading system. Framework agreements have already been entered into with a number of trading partners with specific road maps to be followed and specified time frames by which the negotiations are to be completed. Joint Study Groups have also been set up for examining feasibility of CECA between India-Japan, India-Brazil-South Africa and India-Russia. India and European Commission have also set up a High Level Trade Group (HLTG) as mandated by the India-EU Summit held in New Delhi on September 7, 2005. The mandate of the HLTG is to explore ways and means to increase bilateral economic flows including the possible launching of negotiations on a comprehensive trade and investment agreement.

Look East Policy

East Asia—including Japan, China, South Korea and ASEAN—is today India's largest trading partner, ahead of EU and the US. India unveiled the *Look East* policy in 1991.

Proliferation of Free Trade Agreements (FTAs) is the clearest evidence of Asian countries' desire to forge closer economic relationships. The growing importance of CECA's indicates that such agreements are becoming deeper, extending to areas beyond just tariff reduction.

Intra-regional trade and investment require building up of shared infrastructure. Many Asian countries have joined together to develop cross-border infrastructure to lay the foundations for closer trading relationships and increased connectivity among countries. The Greater Mekong Sub-region is quite advanced in this endeavour. Similar initiatives are underway in South Asia and in Central Asia, with exciting prospects for future development. The spirit of enhanced monetary cooperation in Asia is evident from initiatives like the Chiang Mai Initiative and the Asian Bond Fund having major potential for financing regional investments.

Asia remains one of the least integrated regions lacking a continent-wide regional organization. Forging closer links among Asian nations through appropriate institutional mechanisms can lead to substantial enhancement of national, regional and global productivity and output. In the past, India had adopted a very cautious approach to regionalism, and was engaged in only a few bilateral/regional initiatives, mainly through Preferential Trade Agreements (PTAs).

Recognising that RTAs would continue to feature in world trade for a long time, and with the intention of expanding its export market, India began concluding in principle agreements as a possible step towards CECAs, which cover FTA in goods (zero customs duty regime within a fixed time frame on items covering substantial trade, and a relatively small negative list of sensitive items with no or limited duty concessions), services, investment and identified areas of economic cooperation.

The recently concluded CECA with Singapore was implemented from August 1, 2005. The Agreement on South Asia Free Trade Area (SAFTA) was signed by member countries of South Asian Association for Regional Cooperation (SAARC) in January, 2004. Negotiation on all aspects of SAFTA was concluded recently and the tariff liberalization programme is scheduled to be implemented from July 1, 2006.

Framework Agreement on Comprehensive Economic Cooperation between ASEAN and India, Framework Agreement for Bangladesh, India, Myanmar, Sri Lanka and Thailand Economic Cooperation (BIMSTEC) FTA, and India-Thailand Framework Agreement have also been signed, and FTA on Goods, Services and Investment with BIMSTEC are under negotiation. India-China, India-Japan, and India-South Korea joint study groups have also been set up.

South Asia Free Trade Area (SAFTA)

The Agreement on SAFTA was signed during the 12th SAARC Summit on January 6, 2004 in Islamabad. The tariff liberalisation programme under the Agreement came into force from July 1, 2006.

India, Pakistan and Sri Lanka are categorized as Non-Least Developed Contracting States (NLDCS) and Bangladesh, Bhutan, Maldives and Nepal are categorized as Least Developed Contracting States (LDCS).

Afghanistan which became the eighth member of SAARC during the 14th SAARC Summit held on April 3-4, 2007 in New Delhi is due to become a party to the SAFTA Agreement as an LDC member.

Article 7 of the SAFTA Agreement provides for a phased tariff liberalization programme (TLP) under which, in two years, NLDCS would bring down tariffs to 20 percent, while LDCS will bring them down to 30 percent. Non-LDCS will then bring down tariffs from 20 percent to 0-5 percent in 5 years (Sri Lanka 6 years), while LDCS will do so in 8 years. NLDCs will reduce their tariffs for LDC products to 0-5 percent in 3 years. This TLP would cover all tariff lines except those kept in the sensitive list (negative list) by the member states.

The salient features of the four Annexes of SAFTA Agreement are as under:

Rules of Origin: For giving preferential access to the Member Countries under SAFTA, the goods shall have undergone substantial manufacturing process in the exporting countries. The substantial manufacturing process are defined in terms of twin criteria of Change of Tariff Heading (CTH) at four-digit Harmonized Coding System (HS) and value content of 40% (30% for LDCSs).

Apart from the general rules, to provide for Products-Specific Rules (PSR) for 191 tariff lines to accommodate the interest of LDCSs given their limited base for natural resources and undiversified industrial structure. The Products Specific Rules have been provided clearly on technical grounds i.e. where both inputs and outputs are at the same four-digit HS level.

Mechanism for Compensation of Revenue Loss (MCRL) for the Least Developed Contracting States: The compensation to LDCSs, except to Maldives, would be available for four years; to Maldives it would be for six years. The MCRL to Afghanistan, which is due to become a party to the SAFTA, will also be at par with Maldives.

The compensation would be in the form of grant in US dollar.

The compensation shall be subject to a cap of 1% of customs revenue collected on non-sensitive items under bilateral trade in the base year, i.e. average of 2004 and 2005.

The compensation shall be administered by the SAFTA Committee of Experts as per the Administrative Arrangements.

Technical Assistance to Least Developed Contracting States in Agreed Areas: The main areas covered are capacity building in standards, product certification, training of human resources, data management, institutional upgradations, improvement of legal systems and administration, customs procedures and trade facilitation, market development and promotion.

Implementation of SAFTA Agreement: Tariff Concessions granted under the SAARC Preferential Trading Arrangement (SAPTA) would cease for the LDC Member States once the Non-LDCSs complete the Trade Liberalization Programme (TLP) for LDCSs within three years. If any items, on which SAPTA concessions are available to LDCSs, appear in the Sensitive List of Non-LDCSs, they shall maintain the same level of concessions through derogation under Article 7(3)(a) and indicate the same in their respective Sensitive Lists, and if the items under TLP enjoy tariff preferences under SAPTA, the Non-LDCS shall reduce their tariff on those items to a rate not higher than the rate applicable for LDCS under SAPTA on the date agreed for base rate for TLP.

The base rate for the purpose of tariff reduction would be MFN applied rate existing as on January 1, 2006.

The TLP became operational from July 1, 2006 with the condition that the TLP for the first two years would be completed by December 31, 2007, i.e. within two years of SAFTA coming into force.

India, with a view to providing greater market access to its neighbouring least developed countries, unilaterally reduced tariffs to zero percent for LDCS countries of SAFTA with effect from January 1, 2008 thereby completing the SAFTA tariff liberalization for these countries one year ahead of December 31, 2008 stipulated in the SAFTA Agreement.

The notifications issued by Pakistan for SAFTA tariff concessions have an India specific-rider that Indian imports into Pakistan would continue to be as per their Positive List of importable items from India which at present consists of 1938 item.

India and ASEAN

India's engagement with the Association of South East Asian Nations (ASEAN) started with its *Look East Policy* in the year 1991. ASEAN has a membership of 10 countries, namely Brunei Darussalam, Cambodia, Indonesia, Lao PDR, Malaysia, Myanmar, Philippines, Singapore, Thailand and Vietnam. India became a Sectoral Dialogue Partner of ASEAN in 1992 and Full Dialogue Partner in 1996. In November 2001, the ASEAN-India relationship was upgraded to the summit level.

The 1st ASEAN Economic Ministers (AEM)–India Consultations were held on 15th September 2002 in Brunei Darussalam where the Ministers, after discussing the Joint Study Report decided to establish an ASEAN-India Economic Linkages Task Force (AIELTF). The AIELTF was asked to prepare a draft Framework Agreement to enhance the ASEAN-India trade and economic cooperation before the 2nd AEM–India Consultations. Subsequently, at the First ASEAN-India Summit held on November 5, 2002 in Phnom Penh, Cambodia, the Prime Minister of India made the following major announcements:

- India will extend special and differential trade treatment to ASEAN countries, based on their levels of development to improve their market access to India;
- FTA within 10 years timeframe.

A Framework Agreement on Comprehensive Economic Cooperation between the Association of South East Asian Nations (ASEAN) and India was signed by the Prime Minster of India and the Heads of Nation/Governments of ASEAN members during the Second ASEAN–India Summit on October 8, 2003 in Bali, Indonesia.

The key elements of the Framework Agreement on Comprehensive Economic Cooperation between ASEAN and India cover FTA in goods, services and investment, as well as Areas of Economic Cooperation. The Agreement also provided for an Early Harvest Programme (EHP) which covers areas of Economic Cooperation and a common list of items for exchange of tariff concessions as a confidence building measure.

Presently, the ASEAN-India Trade Negotiating Committee (TNC) is undertaking negotiations for a Comprehensive Economic Cooperation Agreement (CECA) which includes a Free Trade Area in goods, services and investment. Agreement has been reached on the Rules of Origin and Dispute Settlement Mechanism. The TNC is now negotiating the modalities for tariff reduction and elimination.

India-Sri Lanka Free Trade Agreement (ISLFTA)

India-Sri Lanka Free Trade Agreement, signed in December 1998 and in operation since March 2000, provides for tariff reduction/elimination in a phased manner on all items except the negative list and tariff rate quota (TRQ) items. While India has already completed the tariff elimination programme in March 2003, Sri Lanka was scheduled to reach zero duty by 2008.

Now, both sides are in advanced stage of negotiation on having a Comprehensive Economic Partnership Agreement (CEPA) which would encompass trade in goods as well as trade in services and economic cooperation.

India-Thailand Comprehensive Economic Cooperation Agreement (CECA)

In November 2001, the Prime Minister of Thailand, Dr. Thaksin Shinawatra and the Prime Minister of India agreed to set up a Joint Working Group (JWG) to undertake feasibility study on a Free Trade Agreement between India and Thailand. The Joint Working Group observed that the present policy regimes in both the countries were conducive to more intensive bilateral economic integration and a Free Trade Agreement could prove to be a building block for other sub-regional, regional and global economic integration processes of which both countries are a part. Having observed rich potential of trade expansion, the study concluded that the proposed Free Trade Agreement between India and Thailand is feasible, desirable and mutually beneficial. Accordingly, a

Joint Negotiating Group was set up to draft the Framework Agreement on India – Thailand FTA.

During the visit of Indian Prime Minister to Thailand, a Framework Agreement for establishing Free Trade between India and Thailand was signed by the Commerce Ministers of the two sides on October 9, 2003 in Bangkok, Thailand. The Framework Agreement covers FTA in Goods, Services and Investment and Areas of Economic Cooperation. The Framework Agreement also provided for an Early Harvest Scheme (EHS) under which 82 common items of export interest to the sides have been agreed for elimination of tariff on a fast track basis.

The tariff concessions on 82 items of EHS list began from September 1, 2004. The tariffs on these items became zero for both sides from September 1, 2006.

India-Thailand Trade Negotiating Committee (TNC) has been constituted and discussions are being held on the text of FTA, Rules of Origin, Dispute Settlement Mechanism and Sensitive List. 17 Rounds of negotiations for FTA in Goods have so far been held. Negotiations for FTA in Services and Investment have also begun.

The India-Thailand FTA on Trade in Goods is expected to be concluded in 2009.

Bay of Bengal Initiative for Multi-Sectoral Technical and Economic Cooperation (BIMSTEC) Free Trade Agreement (FTA)

The initiative to establish Bangladesh-India-Sri Lanka-Thailand Economic Cooperation (BIST-EC) was taken by Thailand in 1994 to explore economic cooperation on a sub-regional basis involving contiguous countries of South East & South Asia grouped around the Bay of Bengal. Myanmar was admitted in December 1997 and the initiative was renamed as BIMSTEC. It may be mentioned that the initiative involves 3 members of SAARC (India, Bangladesh and Sri Lanka) and 2 members of ASEAN (Thailand, Myanmar). BIMSTEC is visualized as a *bridging link* between two major regional groupings, i.e. ASEAN and SAARC. BIMSTEC is an important element in India's *Look East* strategy and adds a new dimension to our economic cooperation with South East Asian countries.

The 2nd BIMSTEC Summit was held on November 13, 2008 in New Delhi, India. The Summit took place four years after the 1st BIMSTEC Summit in Thailand.

In conclusion, the leaders expressed their satisfaction at the progress that has been made in the negotiations for a Free Trade Agreement in trade in goods and called for their early conclusion. They welcomed the establishment of the Centres for Energy and Weather and Climate in India and the BIMSTEC Cultural Observatory in Bhutan. They also expressed concern at the threat which terrorism poses to the region and satisfaction with the finalization of the BIMSTEC Convention on Combating International Terrorism, Transnational Organized Crime and Illicit Drug Trafficking.

India-Singapore Comprehensive Economic Cooperation Agreement (CECA)

A Joint Study Group (JSG) for establishing a Comprehensive Economic Cooperation Agreement (CECA) between the two countries was set up on April 8, 2002. The JSG submitted its report on April 8, 2003.

The JSG identified areas of increased economic engagement between the two countries and also recommended measures to be taken. The JSG recommended the early launching of negotiations for a CECA to be structured as an integrated package of agreement between India and Singapore including the following:

1. A Free Trade Agreement, which would include, inter alia, trade in goods and services and investment.
2. A bilateral agreement on investment promotion, protection and cooperation.
3. An improved Double Taxation Avoidance Agreement.

4. A more liberal Air Services Agreement and Open Skies for Charter Flights.
5. A work programme of cooperation in a number of areas including health care, education, media, tourism and the creation.

'Declaration of Intent' was signed between the two countries on April 8, 2003. Negotiations on CECA were launched in New Delhi on May 27-28, 2003.

The Comprehensive Economic Cooperation Agreement (CECA) between India and Singapore was signed on June 29, 2005 by the Prime Minister Mr. Manmohan Singh and Mr. Lee Hsien Loong, Prime Minister of Singapore. The CECA has become operational with effect from August 1, 2005.

In December 2007, India granted market access on additional 539 tariff lines through a Protocol amending the India-Singapore CECA.

The implementation of CECA is reviewed regularly at the level of Secretaries.

Asia Pacific Trade Agreement (APTA)

The Asia-Pacific Trade Agreement (APTA), previously named the Bangkok Agreement, signed in 1975 as an initiative of ESCAP, is a preferential tariff arrangement that aims at promoting intra-regional trade through exchange of mutually agreed concessions by member countries. APTA has five members namely Bangladesh, China, India, Republic of Korea, Lao People's Democratic Republic and Sri Lanka. ESCAP functions as the secretariat for the Agreement.

The Second Ministerial Council Meeting of Asia Pacific Trade Agreement (APTA) was held in Goa on October 26, 2007. The Ministerial Council adopted, through the Ministerial Declaration, a common set of "Operational Procedures for the Certification and Verification of the Origin of Goods under the Asia-Pacific Trade Agreement", as recommended by the 27th Session of the Standing Committee and agreed to implement these procedures with effect from January 1, 2008.

The important decisions taken in the Meeting were as follows:

1. An announcement to launch the 4th Round of Negotiations was made. The Standing Committee has been directed to conclude the negotiations by the 3rd Ministerial Council Meeting.
2. The Standing Committee is to adopt modalities for extension of negotiations in other areas such as non-tariff measures, trade facilitation, services, and investment. To this effect the prospects of APTA have been widen by the Ministers.
3. A common set of Operational Procedures for the Certificate and Verification of the Origin of Goods for APTA was approved and it was decided that the same would be implemented w.e.f. January 1, 2008.
4. The Standing Committee and the Secretariat would take necessary action to expand the membership of this Agreement and Member Countries to give positive consideration to support the Secretariat's activities relating to APTA.

To move forward the 4th Round of Negotiations, the APTA sub-regional seminar on February 24, 2009 and 31st Session of the Standing Committee were held on February 25-27, 2009 in Bangkok.

India-Chile Preferential Trade Agreement (PTA)

A Framework Agreement to Promote Economic Cooperation between India and Chile was signed on January 20, 2005. The Framework Agreement envisaged a Preferential Trade Agreement (PTA) between the two countries as a first step. The Framework Agreement also provides for a Joint Study Group to go into the issues relating to a Free Trade Agreement between the two sides.

As a follow up to the Framework Agreement, a PTA was finalized after four rounds of negotiations between the two sides. The last round of negotiations was held in New Delhi in

November 2005. The PTA has two Annexes relating to the list of products on which the two sides have agreed to give fixed tariff preferences to each other and three Annexes relating to the Rules of Origin, Preferential Safeguard Measures and Dispute Settlement Procedures.

The Framework Agreement to Promote Economic Cooperation, signed Between India and Chile on January 20, 2005, provided for a Joint Study Group (JSG) to identify the potential for cooperation between the two sides in trade in goods and services, investments and other areas of economic cooperation. The Terms of Reference for the JSG were finalized during the negotiations held with Chile in June 2005. The Chilean side submitted a draft report of its part of the JSG recommending the feasibility of an FTA between India and Chile.

The first meeting of the Joint Study Group was held during the PTA negotiations in November 2005. The draft reports prepared by Chile and India were discussed during the meeting. Both sides agreed to submit their conclusions and recommendations to their governments for guiding further action on the matter.

India-South Korea Comprehensive Economic Partnership Agreement (CEPA)

On October 6, 2004, India and South Korea agreed to establish a Joint Study Group to take a comprehensive view of bilateral economic linkages between the two countries. In particular, the Joint Study Group (JSG) was mandated with the task of examining the feasibility of a Comprehensive Economic Partnership Agreement (CEPA) between the two countries.

The JSG, composed of Government officials, economists and representatives of business communities of South Korea and India, concluded that a CEPA between Korea and India would provide significant benefits for both countries.

The JSG recommended that the South Korea-India CEPA

should cover, among other things:

1. Trade in goods.
2. Trade in services.
3. Measures for trade facilitations.
4. Promotion, facilitation and liberalization of investment flows.
5. Measures for promoting bilateral economic cooperation in identified sectors.
6. Other areas to be explored for furthering bilateral partnership.

In pursuance to the recommendations of JSG, A Joint Task Force (JTF) composed of Government officials was constituted. Negotiations for a Comprehensive Economic Partnership Agreement between India and Korea commenced on March 23, 2006, and were substantially concluded in the 12th meeting of the Joint Task Force (JTF) held during September 22-25, 2008 in Seoul.

India-Gulf Cooperation Council (GCC) Free Trade Agreement (FTA)

The Gulf Co-operation Council (GCC) is a customs union comprising of Bahrain, Kuwait, Oman, Qatar, Saudi Arabia and United Arab emirates. They are India's third largest trading partners, with exports to this region constituting about 3-4 percent of India's global exports and our imports from this region accounting for over 20 percent of India's global imports.

India is in the process of negotiating a Free Trade Agreement with GCC and the first round of negotiation was held on March 21-22, 2006. Trade in Services and Investment Cooperation as well as General Economic Cooperation is proposed to be synergized with the FTA.

India-Japan Comprehensive Economic Cooperation Agreement (CECA)

During the visit of Prime Minister Koizumi of Japan to

India in April 2005, the Prime Ministers of the two countries directed that the India-Japan Joint Study Group (JSG), be launched by June 2005, to submit its report within a year, focusing on measures required for a comprehensive expansion of trade in goods, trade in services, investment flows and other areas of economic relations between the two countries.

JSG was constituted to focus on measures required for comprehensive expansion of trade in good, trade in services, investment flows and other areas of economic relations between the two countries. The JSG finalized its report which was submitted to the two Prime Ministers at St. Petersburg on July 17, 2006. The JSG recommended that the Governments of Japan and India launch an inter-governmental negotiation to develop an Economic Partnership Agreement (EPA)/ Comprehensive Economic Partnership Agreement (CEPA), within a reasonable period of time. The EPA/CEPA needs to be consistent with WTO provisions, while sensitive sectors should be treated with flexibility and practicality. The JSG also recommended that negotiations on the proposed EPA/CEPA be conducted in a specially-constituted Joint Task Force (JTF), or another mutually agreed suitable mechanism, consisting of government officials. The JTF may consult with the representatives of the business community whenever necessary.

A Joint Ministerial Statement on the launching of a JTF to develop an Economic Partnership Agreement (EPA)/ Comprehensive Partnership Agreement (CEPA) between India and Japan was issued on December 15, 2006 during the Prime Minister's visit to Japan. As per the negotiating structure annexed to the Joint Ministerial Statement the EPA/CEPA negotiations consist of meetings at the chief delegate level and the working level.

Eleven meetings of the JTF have been held so far (four at chief delegate level and seven at the working level). In the fifth meeting of the JTF held during January 8-11, 2008, in India both sides agreed to the modalities of negotiations on market access of Trade in goods.

On investment, IPR, trade in services, custom procedure and other related issues various groups have been constituted for negotiations.

India-Malaysia Comprehensive Economic Cooperation Agreement (CECA)

On December 20, 2004, the Prime Ministers of Malaysia and India agreed to the setting up of a Joint Study Group (JSG) to explore the feasibility of Comprehensive Economic Cooperation Agreement (CECA) between the two countries. In accordance with the mandate granted by the two Prime Ministers, the JSG was duly constituted in March 2005.

The JSG Report was submitted in January 2007 and adopted by both the governments on August 11, 2007.

As per the recommendations of the JSG, negotiations towards India-Malaysia CECA commenced with the first meeting of the TNC(Trade Negotiation Committee) taking place on February 4-5, 2008 in Kuala Lumpur. The TNC agreed to conclude the negotiations by March 2009.

Negotiations are being carried out simultaneously towards Agreements on Trade in Goods, Trade in Services, Investment and other areas of economic cooperation.

India-Mauritius Comprehensive Economic Cooperation and Partnership Agreement (CECPA)

A Joint Study Group (JSG) constituted in November 2003 to study the modalities of the CECPA discussed in detail the complementariness and potential synergies between the two economies and, in its report of November 2004, identified investment, trade in goods and services and general economic cooperation for developing modalities of CECPA.

During his visit to Mauritius from March 30-April 2, 2005, the Prime Minister of India conveyed India's acceptance of the report by the JSG on Comprehensive Economic Cooperation and Partnership Agreement and both sides agreed to set up a high-powered negotiating team for processing and finalizing the recommendations of this report within a twelve-month period. Accordingly, an empowered team was constituted for negotiating a Comprehensive Economic Cooperation and Partnership Agreement (CECPA) with Mauritius. Five rounds of talks have so far been held by the empowered team.

Texts of Preferential Trade Agreement (PTA) and its annexures, viz. Rules of Origin, Operational Certification Procedures and Trade Defence Measures have been finalised.

The following MoUs/Agreements were signed by India and Mauritius in October 2005 under the aegis of CECPA.

1. MOU in the field of Consumer Protection and Legal Metrology.
2. MOU between Bureau of Indian Standards (BIS) and Mauritius Standards Bureau (MSB).
3. MOU between Indian Institute of Public Administration (IIPA) and Government of Mauritius.
4. MOU on Preferential Trade Agreement (PTA).

Negotiations are being held on the liberalization of Trade in Services with a view to creating a more liberal, facilitative, transparent and competitive services regime in the two countries and to strengthen cooperation in services sector.

Issues relating to Financial Services sector, Mutual Recognition Agreements and Movement of Natural Persons are being deliberated upon. Both sides have agreed to explore the possibility of expanding trade in services by synergizing with the Common Market for Eastern and Southern Africa (COMESA) and Southern African Development Community (SADC) markets.

Issues relating to improving the effectiveness of the existing Double Taxation Avoidance Agreement for the mutual benefit of the two countries and review of the existing Bilateral Investment Protection Agreement to enhance its scope and effectiveness are being deliberated upon. Discussions have been held for improving the existing legal framework in both countries in this regard and other issues related to facilitation of investment.

Cooperation in the fields of Health, Standards, SMEs development, Education, Information Technology & Telecommunication, Seafood industry and cooperation between private sectors of the two countries have been deliberated upon for investment, capacity building, training, technology transfer and related activities.

India-SACU Preferential Trade Agreement (PTA) Negotiations

South Africa, Lesotho, Swaziland, Botswana and Namibia have formed the South Africa Customs Union (SACU) with a common Custom Tariff Policy. A Joint Working Group (JWG) consisting of Government representatives from both sides was set up to examine the proposal to prepare a draft Frame Work Treaty for the Preferential Trade Agreement (PTA) between India and SACU countries. In a meeting of JWG held in Namibia on September 6-7, 2004, the draft Framework Agreement was finalized.

The sixth session of the India-South Africa Joint Ministerial Commission Meeting held in New Delhi on December 5-6, 2005. Both sides agreed that a comprehensive Free Trade Agreement within a reasonable time and in the interim, a limited scope agreement providing for exchange of tariff concessions on select list of products, between India and SACU would give further impetus to bilateral trade and urged its early conclusion.

India-Pakistan Trading Arrangement

India and Pakistan have no formal trade agreement. India has granted Most Favoured Nation Status to Pakistan, whereas Pakistan maintains a List of Importable Items from India called 'Positive List' which now consists of 1938 items.

Both countries had constituted a Joint Study Group (JSG) at the level of Commerce Secretary. Its first meeting was held in February 2005 and the last (third meeting) in New Delhi on

August 2, 2007. In this meeting both sides are in the process of discussions to address the issues concerning customs cooperation, sanitary, phyto-sanitary measures and technical barriers to trade, standards and conformance to the extent feasible.

Apart from the JSG, the issues pertaining to commercial and economic cooperation are also discussed at Commerce Secretary level within the framework of the Composite Dialogue. The fourth round of dialogue was held in New Delhi from July 31 to August 1, 2007.

India-Nepal Treaty of Trade

Treaty of Trade: The bilateral trade between India and Nepal is regulated by the Treaty of Trade. The current Treaty has been in force for a period of 5 years with effect from March 6, 2002. Presently, this Treaty was to expire on March 6, 2007. Hence, both Governments of Nepal and India have decided to renew the Treaty in its current form with effect from March 6, 2007.

Both sides are also engaged in mutual consultation process to amend the treaty of trade and once this process is over, the amended Treaty of Trade shall replace the existing Treaty, after necessary approval. Pending completion of the process for its renewal with certain amendments proposed, the validity of the Agreement would continue till a new Treaty comes into force.

Under this Treaty, there is free trade on mutually agreed to primary products from each other as indicated in Protocol to Article IV of the Treaty. In the case of industrial goods produced in Nepal, Article V of the Treaty provides for India to give, on a non-reciprocal basis, duty-free access to Nepalese goods without any quantity restriction. This is subject to fulfilling the twin criterion of four-digit tariff head change and value addition of 30% at ex-factory price in Nepal. This duty-free access is, however, restricted to annual quotas on four sensitive items in the interest of the domestic industries in these sectors. These are vanaspati (one lakh metric tones), Copper products and Acrylic Yarn (Ten thousand metric tones each) and Zinc Oxide (2500 metric tones). The routes for bilateral trade can be mutually decided; in the present Treaty, 22 mutually agreed routes are prescribed for bilateral trade. The Treaty provides for setting up Joint Committee in the event the imports under the Treaty result in injury to the domestic industry in each country.

Treaty of Transit: India provides transit facilities to the landlocked Nepal under the Treaty of Transit. The current Treaty which was renewed in January 2006 would be in force for a period of seven years up to January 5, 2013. This Treaty provides for free movement of traffic-in-transit across territories of each other through mutually agreed routes for trade with third countries subject to taking measures to ensure that this does not infringe legitimate interests/security interests of each other. Traffic in transit is exempted from customs/all transit duties. The Treaty provides for exit/entry points as may be mutually agreed upon. India has allowed 15 transit routes to Nepal but so far not availed of this facility from Nepal. Merchant ships of Nepal are accorded treatment no less favourable than that accorded to ships of any other foreign country. Presently Kolkata/Haldia are the operational entry points for Nepal's trade with third countries. Nepal has requested for similar facilities at Mumbai and Kandla.

Agreement of Cooperation to Control Unauthorized Trade: India and Nepal have also signed an Agreement of Cooperation to Control Unauthorized Trade between the two countries. This Agreement was last renewed for 5 years with effect from March 6, 2007. The objective of this Agreement is to check illegal trade (smuggling) between the two countries.

Inter-Governmental Committee (IGC) at Commerce Secretary-level: Both countries have established a forum known as Inter Governmental Committee at Commerce Secretary-level to address the problems relating to bilateral trade, transit facilities and prevention of Unauthorized Trade which meet as often as required.

India-EU Broad-based Trade and Investment Agreement

On June 28, 2007, India and the EU began negotiations on a broad-based Bilateral Trade and Investment Agreement (BTIA) in Brussels, Belgium.

These negotiations are pursuant to the commitment made by political leaders at the India-EU Summit held in Helsinki on October 13, 2006 to move towards negotiations for a broad-based trade and investment agreement. India and the EU expect to promote bilateral trade by removing barriers to trade in goods and services and investment across all sectors of the economy. Both parties believe that a comprehensive and ambitious agreement that is consistent with WTO rules and principles would open new markets and would expand opportunities for Indian and EU businesses. To achieve this objective, six rounds of negotiations have been alternately held at Brussels and New Delhi respectively, the 6th Round was held during March 17-19, 2009. The negotiations cover Trade in Goods, Trade in Services, Investment, Sanitary and Phytosanitary Measures, Technical Barriers to Trade, Rules of Origin, Trade Facilitation and Customs Cooperation, Competition, Trade Defence mechanism, Government Procurement, Dispute Settlement, IPR & GIs.

India-European Free Trade Association (EFTA) Negotiations on Broad-based Bilateral Trade and Investment Agreement

EFTA comprises Switzerland, Iceland, Norway and Liechtenstein. These countries are not part of the European Union (EU). Recognizing the need for enhancing bilateral trade, a Joint Study Group (JSG) between India and EFTA was established and mandated to take a comprehensive view of bilateral economic linkages between India and EFTA, covering among other, trade in goods and services, investment flows, and other areas of economic cooperation, and to examine the feasibility of a bilateral broad based trade and investment agreement.

Based on the conclusions of JSG, negotiations commenced in October 2008 for the India-EFTA broad-based trade and investment agreement. Three rounds of negotiations have been held so far.

Global System of Trade Preferences (GSTP)

The Agreement establishing the Global System of Trade Preferences (GSTP) among Developing countries was signed on April 13, 1988 at Belgrade following conclusion of the First Round of Negotiations. The GSTP came into being after a long process of negotiations during the Ministerial Meeting of the Group of 77, notably at Mexico City in 1976, Arusha in 1979, and Caracas in 1981. The Ministers of Foreign Affairs of the Group of 77 in New York set up the GSTP Negotiating Committee in 1982. The New Delhi Ministerial meetings, held in July 1985, gave further impetus to the GSTP negotiation process. The Brasilia Ministerial Meeting held in May 1986 launched the First Round of GSTP Negotiations. At the conclusion of the First Round in April 1988 in Belgrade, the GSTP Agreement was signed on April 13, 1988. The Agreement entered into force on April 19, 1989. 44 countries have ratified the Agreement and have become participants.

The GSTP establishes a framework for the exchange of trade concessions among the members of the Group of 77. It lays down rules, principles and procedures for conduct of negotiations and for implementation of the results of the negotiations. The coverage of the GSTP extends to arrangements in the area of tariffs, para-tariff, non-tariff measures, direct trade measures including medium and long-term contracts and sectoral agreements. One of the basic principles of the Agreement is that it is to be negotiated step by step improved upon and extended in successive stages.

Index

Index